Healing Through
the Shadow of Loss

Healing Through the Shadow of Loss

DEBORAH MORRIS CORYELL

Healing Arts Press
Rochester, Vermont

Healing Arts Press
One Park Street
Rochester, Vermont 05767
www.InnerTraditions.com

Healing Arts Press is a division of Inner Traditions International

*Note to the reader: This book is intended as an informational guide. The remedies,
approaches, and techniques described herein are meant to supplement, and not to
be a substitute for, professional medical care or treatment. They should not be used
to treat a serious ailment without prior consultation with a qualified health care
professional.*

Library of Congress Cataloging-in-Publication Data
Coryell, Deborah Morris.
  [Good grief]
  Healing through the shadow of loss / Deborah Morris Coryell.
    p. cm.
  Originally published: Good grief. Santa Fe, N.M. : Shiva Foundation,
c1997.
  ISBN 0-89281-197-8 (pbk.)
  1. Grief. 2. Bereavement—Psychological aspects. 3. Death—Psychological
aspects. 4. Loss (Psychology) I. Title.
  BF575.G7C68 2004
  155.9'37—dc22
                                                    2004003632

Printed and bound in Canada at Webcom

10 9 8 7 6 5 4 3 2 1

Text design by The Warren Group
This book was typeset in Garamond with Bernhard Modern and Nuptial
Script as the display typefaces

*This book is dedicated
to my father, Saul Goldman (of blessed memory),
an ordinary man whose extraordinary love
continues to teach me and heal me.*

—————— *With Gratitude* ——————

Through the agonies and ecstasies of writing this book, I have been inspired by guardian angels. My journey into healing through grief would not have been possible without the unconditional love and financial support of Phyllis and Harvey Sandler, Marsha and Ben Swirsky, and Carolyn and Steve Lieberman. By providing the means of support, they gave me so much more of myself. I am eternally grateful.

I am grateful to my "family": Carl and Freya Diamond, Blair Sabol, Doris Ober, Andy Weil, Karma Kientzler, and Joseph Barbera who "just" believed in me—when I stumbled, fell, doubted, and raged, they held steady. They knew better than me, at times, what it was that I needed to do.

I am grateful to Jane Centofante whose editing brought divine order out of sacred chaos; to Mindy Seeger who brought me Jane and whose soulful listening carried me across some very rough spots; and to Annette Hanzer Pfau who read these words with her heart and then designed a beautiful book to hold them.

I am grateful to my husband Bill, my soul's mate, who took page after page of illegible script—arrows shooting front to back and top to bottom—and painstakingly constructed not one, not two, but three versions of this book; who shared with me some terrifying descents into a lifetime of grief; who inspires me with his love.

I am grateful to my son Matt whose birth gave me someone to live for and whose life continues to humble and teach me, day by day.

And last, I am grateful to all those whose deaths brought their grieving families and friends to me; who taught me that grief is the birthright of life and that love doesn't need a form, it just needs an open heart.

Life can only be understood backwards;
but it must be lived forwards.

SØREN KIERKEGAARD

Contents

Letter to the Reader

I want to unfold,
I don't want to stay folded anywhere,
because where I am folded,
there I am a lie . . .

RAINER MARIA RILKE

Gentle Reader,

It was 1985 when I received the first phone call that drew me into the circle of grief. As Director of the Wellness/ Education Program at Canyon Ranch Spa in Tucson, Arizona, I thought I had gotten where I was going. Having been a part of the team that envisioned this magnificent environment committed to health, education, and fitness, creating the Wellness Department seemed to be the culmination of what, at that point, had been my life's work.

As a little girl growing up in Brooklyn, New York, I had discovered the seduction of teaching. One of my earliest memories comes from the fourth grade when our teacher was explaining something in social studies class that my friend couldn't seem to understand. I leaned over to explain what it was the teacher was saying and saw, with amazement, the look of confusion and fear on my friend's face turn into the relief of comprehension. I was hooked! Years later my father would perfect the art of sleeping with his eyes open so that I could use him as my audience for all that I was learning and so desperate to teach.

When Ron Sandler, then general manager of Canyon Ranch, called me to the phone in 1985 to ask if I would speak to a woman whose teenage son had committed suicide two weeks prior, I didn't hesitate. Of course I would, I answered, having no idea what I would say. When Gloria got on the phone I could barely hear her voice. In a whisper, she asked: "What can we possibly talk about? How can you help me?" I surprised both of us by saying it was her son Robert who needed help—Robert who needed healing. "But he's dead," his mother wept. Yes. Then we would need to go to where he is . . . in our hearts and in our minds.

At that moment, my life turned a corner. I could not know it then, nothing had changed very much. I continued as director of the spa's Wellness/Education Program until we outgrew each other. Then I turned my focus exclusively to counseling those dealing with catastrophic life events. Every so often a mother would come to me bearing her burden, grieving for her dead child. My heart broke open with each one. My work with catastrophic illness had brought me to the gateway of life and death many times to share the burden and grieve with the one who was dying. During that time, and even now, when people hear about this work they look at me and wonder about the tragedy of these encounters. I rush to explain. It is an incredible healing for me and a great honor to sit with people and share the burden of grief we all must carry at certain moments in our lives and so often alone. Grieving takes us to the very heart of life itself. Grieving takes us to love and to loss. We only grieve for that which we have loved and, the nature of life being transitory, love and loss are intimately connected. Not only are we all going to die—which we can see as loss of life or as a wave of transforming energy—but every moment is changing and as it changes it brings loss.

My first encounter as a young student with philosophy was with the teaching of the Greek philosopher Heraclitus: "All things change . . . Nothing remains . . . You can never step in the same river twice." What was Heraclitus saying? And was it a cause for celebration or a cause for tears and fears? There is a story that the great physician/analyst Carl Jung would say to a patient suffering in the pits of despair: "Let's open a bottle of champagne! You are at bottom, now we can begin to climb up and out!" But if a patient would come in celebrating and joyous, he would put his head in his hands and say: "Ach! This is terrible. For now the descent will come." This is not Jung's pessimism. It's life. Constantly changing and unpredictable.

At the moment that Gloria and I began our explorations into

what healing might look like for a woman whose son had committed suicide, both of our lives had a certain focus and integrity. Within five years, that picture would totally change for me. I would find myself leaving a home and a community that I never thought I would leave; that I would never have chosen to leave if the force of circumstances hadn't compelled me. The betrayals I struggled to integrate would ultimately mean the loss of not only home, friends, and security, but of my self as I had come to know me.

∾

In childhood, my adored older brother Warren enlisted me in his commitment to medicine. He was going to be a doctor and I would be his nurse. I couldn't imagine anything better and so the twin services of teaching and healing came into my world early and have continued to this day—almost half a century later.

Coming of age in the 1960s, two things happened to set me on my own course. The first was my exposure to the works of such health advocates as Adelle Davis, Carlton Fredericks, Jethro Kloss, and Henry Bieler. Here was a kind of medicine that made sense to the young hippie I was becoming. There seemed to be an innate wisdom and a rightfulness of personal responsibility vis-à-vis one's health and well-being that I could not find in orthodox medicine. Secondly, the early stirrings of feminism and my explorations into yoga, as well as into spiritual dimensions outside of the Jewish orthodoxy in which I had been raised, were beckoning me. I didn't need to be my brother's disenfranchised nurse, I could have my own arena that would honor the passion I was feeling for teaching myself and others how to take care of our own well-being without being wholly dependent on doctors. I began to study yoga and nutrition in earnest, even as I continued to pursue an undergraduate degree in psychology and then graduate studies in social work.

These explorations resulted in a distancing from my family both physically and philosophically, taking its toll on me as it did with so many of my peers in the 1960s. I became alienated from my family and conventional society and began to doubt my ability to survive, much less succeed in the world. By my senior year at Queens College, I was diagnosed with a clinical depression. I called it a nerve-less breakdown. Quite simply, I had lost my nerve and all the confidence and well-being that goes with it. Those were the days when the early discoveries in antidepressants and mood elevators were coming to the fore.

My brother Warren, who by then had completed a PhD in psycho-pharmacology, was attending medical school. He took me to see Helen Singer Kaplan, an enormously creative, compassionate, warm woman who happened to be not only one of his professors but a pioneer in psychiatry at the time. I was put on a series of drugs culminating in Thorazine (now reserved almost exclusively for the treatment of psychosis) and told that I had a chemical imbalance of the brain and, like a diabetic with insulin, would need to take this drug for the rest of my life and all would be well. A few days after my system acclimated to the Thorazine, I began to recover my nerve and began building the foundation of my relationship to myself and to my world. Brick by brick.

As dark and terrifying as that year of my life was, I have always been grateful for the descent. For I found my way back, ultimately without drugs, one step at a time and have always felt that I could never get totally lost again. I would remember the path; like Hansel and Gretel, I had left markers along the way.

My work in healing and grief would eventually lead to my own confrontation with death. In 1981, I discovered a malignant tumor in my throat that proved to be a thyroid cancer that had metastasized into two lymph nodes. At that point, my focus on diet, exercise, and emotional well-being had begun to take a decidedly different turn. I became fascinated by what I was coming to know as the metaphorical equivalence of disease, or the idea that diseases do not come arbitrarily but are a function of how we take care of ourselves as well as how we think and feel about ourselves. The organs that are affected become metaphors for the healing that needs to take place as part of the disease encounter. By example, doctor-author Michael Crichton did some research in the 1970s with heart patients, simply asking each of them why they thought they had had a heart attack. Quite astonishingly to Crichton, each of them spoke of some "heart-break" in their lives! For me, my cancer had begun in the thyroid gland and metastasized to two nearby lymph nodes in the throat. A healer with whom I worked asked me about my lifestyle. At that point, my career was moving at warp-speed, I had a newborn baby and was teaching about self-care. I was eating fast food and racing through each day with no time for anything but work. The healer looked at me and said: "Your mouth is full of sand. You are teaching what you are no longer living." Harsh words but true. I had my surgery to remove the tumor and went about changing my life. Taking time, I began working with cancer patients as well as those dealing with other life-threatening illnesses. Catastrophe became my calling card.

It was only natural, then, in my evolution as a teacher and healer that I would eventually come to embrace the long-held grief of separation from my family. And it truly has been an embrace. When I walked out of my parents' home at nineteen, I walked away from my mother, my brothers, my nieces, and nephews. My gift and my grace was that my father always stood and continues, even in death, to stand by my side.

In 1975, I met a psychiatrist with whom I shared my anguish at having no family. Although I understood the price of my life choices and willingly agreed to pay it, I still suffered deeply the loss of my family. He said to me: "Your people, the Jews, have the healthiest *healing model for grief. Go to it." I was twenty-nine years old at the time and newly divorced, having just moved twenty-seven hundred miles from everyone and everything I knew. I took in what he had to say. Four years later, as I began to develop the Wellness Department at Canyon Ranch Spa in Tucson, I found myself sharing bits and pieces of that ancient wisdom. Along the way, there was much I was taught, mostly by the women who have come through my life "bearing" their grief. I used to wonder at that—why always women?—but I have come to appreciate that aspect of the feminine that can labor through not only birth but also grief.*

In 1990, I moved to Southern California and became involved with a number of wellness center projects but my heart wasn't in it. I went back to graduate school thinking I would join the ranks of licensed clinical therapists. Halfway through my degree, I encountered the profound limitations I had always struggled against in clinical settings, especially the ways in which the client and therapist are locked apart from each other in an effort to protect them from the twin contaminations of intimacy and social intercourse. It was not my way. All through those years from 1985 and that first phone call with Gloria, I had continued to walk the mourner's path with those who found me. The work became a "calling." Side by side, together, we shared what we each were learning from the other. It was a gift to me to be called into arenas that I can only describe as mystical.

After leaving graduate school, I spent some time on the East Coast with three women, all of whom were dealing with some form of grief. Lois, whom I had known for almost fifteen years, was newly diagnosed with a brain tumor that would eventually bring her into her death; Eli, the mother of a dear friend, also newly diagnosed with a brain tumor; and Estelle, whose husband and soul mate had recently died unexpectedly and who was herself so clearly dismembered. When I walked with Estelle, whom I had never met before, into the home she and her husband, Al, had shared, I saw Al's face grinning at me from the photos on the piano. I knew then that I was where I was supposed to be. As I looked into Estelle's ravaged face, I asked aloud: "You must be wondering who I am? Why I am sitting here?" The answer was simple. In the great tradition of Judaism, I was there to "sit" with this family. To share the burden of their grief for as long as I could. Others would come before and after me. We would share, as a community, the task of grieving.

On the flight back home, I turned to my husband, Bill, and said, "This work makes my heart sing." Does that seem strange to you? Death, grief, suffering. How can a healthy person possibly choose to (voluntarily) enter these ranges and say that it makes her heart sing? Is it a morbid preoccupation with death? Is it a vicarious power trip? Neither. For me, it takes me to the very edge of life. To accompany anyone through the valley of the shadow of loss, is to love them and be loved in the most unconditional way. It is to begin to penetrate, however slightly, the mysteries of life and love. It is to meet the demons of fear and the terrifying darkness of the unknown. It is to share the knowledge, for brief seconds at a time, that nothing which we have once known is ever lost.

And so, on that plane with my husband, The Shiva Foundation was born. "Shiva" not only reminds us of the Jewish custom of grieving, but also of Lord Shiva, the representation in Hinduism of life's essential duality: the cycle of birth and death, creation and destruction, one following the other in an endless dance. With The Shiva Foundation, we are exploring the possibilities of healing through grief; of learning a language with which we can communicate our griefs; of having images for loss that open us to the unknown instead of shutting us down in terror; of having ways to think about death and the myriad losses in each day of our lives so that we can ultimately realize the only real loss is our unwillingness to engage life. In *his book* The Heart of Stillness, *David Cooper tells us: "The unknown is a territory where truth is hidden." Healing through our grief asks us, demands of us, that we find our truth.*

On the following pages I offer what I have been taught by all those who have invited me to share their burden of grief. I offer up the teachings so that each is a complete exploration into some aspect of the nature of loss. I trust that it will serve you and help you to find your truths that have been hidden in the unknown.

—Deborah Morris Coryell

Explorations into the Nature of Loss

part one

Being Lost

The journey of ten thousand miles begins under our feet.

TAO TE CHING

I CONFESS. I'M ADDICTED TO MEANING. I search for meaning in seemingly random events, thoughts, images, and, especially, words. So, when I hear that A has lost her husband or B has lost his job, I wonder why we use the word "lost." We could say dead or fired or betrayed but we don't. Mostly we say lost. What then are we really saying when we choose this word above all others? When I first began to think about this question, I believed the choice of the word "lost" was a form of denial or, worse, cowardice. I thought it to be a reflection of our fear and unwillingness to call a spade a spade. I set out, then, to make it wrong to use the word lost. Instead, I have learned how right this particular word is! Because "lost" has levels of meaning that both embrace the physical realms of loss and transcend it to include realms of emotion, thought, and spirit.

Within the idea of "lost" is the feeling of being alone. Are we saying "I have lost" and really meaning "I am lost"? When we are attached to someone or something and we become unattached, we lose our sense of being connected; of knowing where our place is in the world. We've lost our place. Whether it is temporarily lost or permanently lost is up to us. Part of the task of grieving is finding our place in the world again. Who am I if not Jim's wife? Laura's mom? Bob's daughter? Suzanne's friend? Head of the maintenance department? Owner of a beautiful home?

The issues of ownership and responsibility are intrinsic to the idea of "lost." To lose something, it has to be yours. And if it's yours and you've lost it, were you irresponsible? Did you not take care of it? You lose something when you're not paying attention to where you put it. What is meant, then, when one says: "I've lost my husband"? If your husband has been lost, where did you lose him? What exactly *is* lost? Our experience of the world comes to us through our senses. We know our world because we can see it, hear it, taste it, feel it, and smell it. When someone or something or some moment is lost, we lose our ability to sense it.

Our first reaction to loss is visceral and convulsive. We feel as if we've been punched in the belly. We double over, crumple inward, in an effort to ward off the blow. Where is our beloved? Lost to us. We can't find him or her. Because we can't find them, we won't believe it. What the eye can't see, the mind won't comprehend! The shocked disbelief of the first day, the physical revulsion we feel, quickly turns into a torrent of emotion. Loss now deluges us with feelings of guilt. Was I careless? Did I not take care of this gift entrusted to me? What could I have done to prevent this? And now feelings of guilt give way to thoughts of blame—whose fault was this?—and punishment: I've lost it and now I'm being punished. Why me? Why now? Who is to blame? Circling the questions endlessly, exhausted, falling apart, we begin to hear the cry of the spirit: I am what has been lost! Where am I? Who am I? Nothing looks or feels right. Amidst the pain and guilt and anger of loss, we hear the voice of our own soul wandering, lost and beyond our reach.

As children setting off on our own, maybe to the park or the circus, didn't our parents tell us that if we got lost, stay put? Don't go anywhere. Stand still and someone will find you. Forest rangers warn us against panicking and trying to find a lost path in the woods. Stop. Make yourself as comfortable as you can and listen. If you find the right path, set out again. If not, wait. Call for help! There is a wonderful line in the children's classic *Paddington Bear*, where Paddington is in need of assistance and, being a very polite bear, he calls out in a small quiet voice so as not to disturb anyone.

Call out. Disturb the silence with your soul's cry. Your pain, your loss, your grief disturbs our world. The forces of chaos and destruction have been unleashed. When we stop, sit, and listen, we acknowledge not only our loss but the fact that we *are* lost! Among observant Jews the practice of sitting shiva after the death of a family member honors the need for the one who is lost to stop, to sit still for seven (sheva in Hebrew) days. The seven days of shiva begin a year-long cycle of grieving that honors the way our lives are circumscribed by cycles of time; the day, the week, the month, the year. These four cycles can be likened to the four worlds of the physical, the emotional, the mental, and the spiritual. In grieving, we go through the first full cycle of time, the first day, week, month, and year as if each moment is a totally new experience lived for the first time with our loss. By taking the first two cycles—the first day and the first week—to stop, to sit, to step away from the responsibilities and ordinariness of our lives, we can make a space for our lost selves.

For the first two cycles of grief, the physical and emotional, we are in a safe place at home, inside, surrounded by family and friends who care for us. We, who are lost and waiting to be found, can be protected from business concerns and the usual flow of day to day living. Those who have been lost before and know the way can come and escort us back onto the path of the living. But in the beginning we give all our time to allow the pain, the demons, the fears, and the angers to arise. At the end of the week, we step outside to begin our lives again knowing that we still have ahead of us fifty-one weeks to meet as newborns.

Physically, we are dependent on our senses. When someone or something is lost to us, we need to adapt to the sensory changes in our world. Visualization techniques can help us to see, hear, taste, smell, touch all within the mind. The mind's capacity to store experiences and bring them back to us in their full intensity rivals any computer that has yet been imagined. The capacity to nourish ourselves with our memories is vastly underrated, as is the ability of the mind to store for us all of our sense memories. They can never be "lost." When we want or need to be with someone or something we feel disconnected from, we can call upon our stores of remembered experience. Yes, it is different, yet we don't have to judge whether it is worse or better than having the "real thing." With patience and practice, we can simply acknowledge that it's different and learn to appreciate what is now possible. William Brugh Joy, MD, author and teacher of healing consciousness, would say that from a biochemical stand-point, the organism's experience of being hugged by the self is no different than being hugged by another. In hugging one's self the same rise in T cells, immune response, and endorphins are experienced. Similarly, we are learning that the body's response to "imagined" events is often very close to its responses to "real" events.

Focusing on what is not possible, focusing on what is absent in our lives, as opposed to what is present, keeps us caught in a cycle of fear and despair that often manifests itself as anger and blame. We can understand that the emotional defense against fear is anger and the defense against despair is blame. Our psychological survival mechanism—only the strong survive—will take our fear and turn it into anger. Anger is proactive, focusing outward against another, as opposed to fear, which is reactive and aiming inward toward oneself. Despair is transmuted into blame for much the same reason: To turn the focus of attention off of one-self and onto someone else. While this mechanism might be effective in some circumstances, it is a poor and inefficient healing mechanism in the face of grief and loss. Why? Because we have more power over ourselves than we have over another. I can choose to change my mind but I can't choose to change yours. To take my fear and despair and make it someone else's fault is to disempower myself. Likewise, to take my fear and despair and turn it into anger and blame directed inward is to disempower myself. If I can't turn it outward and I can't turn it inward, what can I do? The only choice remaining is to meet my fear and despair honestly and with as much support from the world around me as I can call upon.

After sitting shiva for seven days, we walk outside on the eighth day, surrounded by family knowing that we walk the path of one who is lost. We know now that the loss has dismembered us and that we are walking the path of remembering. Loss is the physical and mental experience. Grieving is the process of moving into the emotional and spiritual realms that the months and years ahead offer to us. Healing is a journey, not a destination.

Core Grief

... each loss somehow echoes that first loss,
the one we know so well.
Something falls into place,
so familiar it is almost a relief.

GLORIA VANDERBILT, *A MOTHER'S STORY*

I HAVE HEARD IT SAID that in the first stages of grief we have all these feelings and no container for them. No place to hold the feelings. Over time I have learned that grief *is* the container. Grief holds all of the feelings and thoughts and pictures that we experience in our encounters with loss. Some native cultures actually create vessels—a pot, a basket, or a bowl—that symbolically contain one's grief. With such a vessel a person can put her grief away and know that it is safe and available at any time. Rituals and ritual objects are painfully absent in our culture at every level and nowhere felt to be as powerfully absent as in times of loss.

I have come to believe that there is a "core grief" inside each of us. That, indeed, we are born with a grief at the very center of our being. With grief being the container for loss, we are each born with that container at our very core since birth itself represents loss, the loss of union. At birth, we lose our union with mother. We disconnect from the source of life that has held us and protected us for the first nine months. For some, birth represents the loss of our union with the Divine. And we are born, I believe, with the knowledge of our own mortality: the organism knows, at a cellular level, of its eventual death. Cells are dying from the moment of birth.

If grief is born with us, and we are the container, why aren't we more familiar with grief? Our bodies contain our grief. Perhaps children know this and therefore have a facility with loss that adults deny. They cry easily over loss and are quickly healed. We say it's because they don't comprehend the significance of loss—maybe it's because they do comprehend! They are closer to it. They have already suffered the greatest loss in life: expulsion from the safety and bliss of the mother's womb. We have been given the basic teaching right at birth. It is a lifelong lesson: how to go on living and loving and growing in consciousness in the face of separation from the loved object.

Grief is then not something outside of us, extrinsic to our nature. It is contained within us. It is intrinsic to us. We know, in the Biblical sense of knowing, how to grieve. We are intimate with it. When we don't honor a loss by acknowledging it, first to ourselves and then to our familiars, the grief accumulates. We suppress our feelings until a loss comes along that's big enough to knock us off our feet. And now all the suppressed losses come flowing out adding to the pain of this particular moment. Now we can be truly overwhelmed.

When D's daughter died of a heart attack at age twenty-five, she was faced not only with the death of her child but also with the responsibility for her young grandchildren. One day as we spoke on the telephone, she began to talk about her anger at her ex-husband for the divorce they had been through six years before. Why now, she wondered? Because her daughter's death had broken her open and all that was held inside was beginning to come out.

As a society, we tend to judge and rank our losses. We have decided that the grief we meet when someone we love dies is the "worst" grief. Although even here there is a hierarchy of grief. Grieving for a child is the greatest grief, we say; who will come next? A parent? A spouse? A sibling? What of friends who have become like family?

Under the umbrella of loss we are beginning to include the grief that comes when families and friends separate through circumstances other than death. In our incredibly mobile society, grief comes as a result of divorce or a move from city to city or even from one neighborhood to another. What about the grief we feel for lost youth and dreams that are not realized? Watching sporting events, we hear so much of the long, hard road to a single moment in a young athlete's life that will or won't be realized. At the 1996 Olympic games, when American swimmer Janet Evans failed in her attempt to win one of her events, the media descended upon her seconds after her loss. Evans was incredibly true to her own grief when she not only asked for, but demanded, some time to "be" with her loss. She resisted the reporter's timetable to "get on" with it. At such times there is a tendency to say: "But you still have your life ahead of you. It is not as bad a grief as dying." In that moment there is a death! The death of the person she would have been had she attained her dream. And it is a death that needs to be mourned in its own right and on its own terms.

The violent, sudden death of a young person is commonly held to be a loss most worthy of long and deep grieving. The loss least worthy of prolonged grief is thought to be for an elderly person who had a good life and died peacefully. But if grief is the container for our experience of loss, how can one be better or worse than another? We each meet the grief that is ours in the moment that it arrives. Comparing and judging one grief over another separates us on the path we all walk. Grief is an experience we share as human beings. Birth, death, and grief are the only life processes every single one of us encounters.

The primary task of healing, therefore, is not to disconnect from each other and from life. When we disconnect we become overwhelmed and are at our lowest ebb. We can only deal with survival—and sometimes not even that. When we are overwhelmed, it is difficult to think clearly or hear what is being said to us. We are lost and at the mercy of our environment. Healing asks us to be present, conscious, and aware.

By paying attention to the "little" losses inherent in each day, we come to be more in tune with our responses to life's "bigger" losses. We have the opportunity to learn about loss. How we respond to the loss of a pet or a friendship teaches us how to deal with other losses. Learning that life is constantly changing and how to let go of our (sometimes) obsessive attachments, a little bit at a time, makes the process of losing familiar. It becomes part of the rhythm of life from which we have become woefully disconnected.

One of the wisdom teachings of grief is that we are all connected in our experience of loss. Just at the moment when we feel the pain of separation from the one we love or the place we love, we are connected to every single person who ever has or ever will experience a similar loss. Life and loss are born within each of us. We know grief yet we shun it and shun those around us whose grief is too painful for us to share. Instead of protecting ourselves from "their" grief, we ensure that we too will be pariahs when our grief inevitably surfaces.

The Sufi poet Rumi says: "Be thirst searching for water." What would it take to be loss searching for grief?

Time Does Not Heal All Wounds

In studying the way, realizing it is hard;
once you have realized it, preserving it is hard;
when you can preserve it,
putting it into practice is hard.

ZEN SAYING

AMONG THE MOST FREQUENTLY REPEATED PHRASES about suffering is that "time heals all wounds" or "this too shall pass." Time passes. It does not heal. Healing is an active process not a passive one. If we have a cut and do nothing to clean it out or do not apply a salve, it will probably still form a scab. It might take longer and first develop an infection but the wound will most likely close and leave a scar.

When I was about five years old I ran away from home. I didn't get very far; the downstairs vestibule. I waited what seemed like an eternity for someone to come looking for me. When no one did, I put my hand through one of those small decorative panes of glass in the door. A little sliver of glass was left in the soft fleshy part of my hand. It closed up with that glass inside.

When we experience woundings to our heart, soul, and mind, it feels as if we have been torn open. Sometimes we are bleeding, figuratively, from every orifice of our bodies. Eventually the bleeding stops and the wound closes, but what has closed inside? Have we healed or just closed up with our anger, fear, resentment, and doubt inside? Occasionally we develop a "weeping wound," which doctors define as a wound that doesn't heal because of noxious matter that continues to fester and ooze. How many "weeping wounds" can we contain before our entire system becomes infected?

As we begin to explore the meaning of healing through loss, we come upon the ancient spiritual roots of the healing arts. From prehistoric time, the healer or shaman was the most powerful teacher and wise one of the clan. In many languages, the word "to heal" comes from the word "to be whole," an etymological root derived from the belief that when we become sick, we lose our wholeness. Something or someone has broken through our wholeness and caused dis-ease within our body. To heal is to come back into that lost wholeness. Returning to wholeness often means that we must somehow integrate the disease so it is no longer identified as a threat. Once it is part of us, we have incorporated what was thought to be a threat into our hearts and souls and minds. This explains how it is possible for someone with an incurable illness to be healed—they can use the disease as a path into wholeness. My friend Philomena lived twenty-one months past the three-month life span doctors had given her. In those two years she reached out to find her healing and possibly her cure. She searched for all those places inside where she felt "not whole" and eventually became the person she always wanted to be. Her last words to me were: "If the price of this illness was learning all I've learned, I gladly pay with my life because I've become the person I always wanted to be."

. Healing and curing are two very different concepts. Healing is a spiritual idea and curing is a medical one. Healing is an active process. It doesn't happen to us; we must participate in the process of our healing. Healing happens for us. It is a gift we give to ourselves in the moment we decide to stay "open" to that which has broken us.

In pain management used for patients with chronic pain, it is taught not to tighten around the pain but to relax and allow the pain to be present. The idea is that when pain is resisted, it intensifies. When we breathe deeply and acknowledge the presence of pain, it has room to move and can dissipate more readily. Pain is there to tell us something, to warn us of possible danger. This is as true for emotional, spiritual, and mental pain as it is for physical pain. When pain speaks, we need to listen. All it takes is paying attention to our pain so that when it comes we remember to breathe and get soft. We don't want to fight with our pain. We want to learn from it.

Time does not heal. But healing does take time. Give yourself the gift of time. To become whole means that as we open to the pain, we open to the loss. We break open and, as a consequence, we get bigger and include more of life. We include what would have been "lost" to us if our hearts and minds had closed against the pain. We include what would have been lost if we had not taken the time to heal. As singer/songwriter Carly Simon tells us: "There's more room in a broken heart."

Daily Practice

You cannot discover new oceans
unless you have the courage
to lose sight of the shore.

TIBETAN PROVERB

THE MOST POTENT MESSAGE OUR CULTURE puts out about grief and loss is not to think about it until you absolutely have to! Not only is it one of the first messages we hear but it is one of the most voluble and the most persistent. Not allowing ourselves to think about the possible losses in our lives makes a monster out of grief. We haven't tried it on; we haven't developed any flexibility or resourcefulness about it. We have buried it in our unconscious minds with a heavy topsoil that screams "Danger—Toxic Material!" And what usually accompanies such a sign? A skull-and-crossbones—a symbol of death!

This perspective inspires in us a number of not only unhealthy attitudes towards loss but keeps loss associated with death. Sex, birth, death, and money have all come out of the closet; topics that had been taboo in "polite" society have now become, if not easy, at least accessible topics of conversation. Yet loss and its attendant, grief, continue to be taboo, shameful and hidden. It, like sex, birth, death, and money, is a part of our daily lives. Yes, daily lives. Is there a day that goes by where we don't experience a loss of some kind or another? Perhaps we need to exercise the "muscles" that are used in grieving just like we need to exercise the muscles in our physical bodies. There are levels of fitness and wellness we need to achieve in our attitudes and in our beliefs about this experience called life that can't be postponed.

Our capacity to let go, to lose, with grace and awareness and honor comes from having developed certain skills. Each day presents us with the opportunities to hone those skills. Perhaps it is in the face of a thought that randomly crosses our minds or a story that comes to our attention. Perhaps we are reading a news-paper and come across an account of an accident in which a young man or woman has been killed in a carjacking. Our thoughts immediately seize on this story and transpose it into our own lives. And, just as quickly, we shut it off. No! We won't allow ourselves to think about it! Why not? Are we afraid of becoming morbidly obsessed with "bad" things happening? Do "bad" things not happen because we won't allow ourselves to think about them?

A popular contemporary self-help book is entitled *When Bad Things Happen To Good People*—my second reaction to that title was: Who should they happen to? Can we all agree on a group of people we will call on to carry all the tragedies? My first reaction was: These are not "bad" things that happen to us. They are events that happen in the course of life itself. As a popular bumper sticker puts it: "Shit happens." How we deal with "shit" is a manifestation of our relative wellness. Loss happens. Lift those light weights of loss that life brings us regularly so that we can see where our strengths and weaknesses lie—where we are injured perhaps and need healing—before we are asked to lift the heavier and heavier weights.

When I sit with someone who asks, "Why me?" I always want to ask, "Why not you?" And if it's not you right now, it will eventually be you. And if it's not this loss it will be some other loss. Is it possible to strengthen those muscles that support us in the face of loss? Absolutely. Strength comes by practicing with each loss that life brings to us. Daily practice occurs by noticing how we deal with a lost earring, a broken leg, or a broken date; by examining our fears and resistances as they arise; by paying attention to the little voices in our minds that say: I would never be able to deal with _____ *(fill in the blank)*. I couldn't go on living without _____ *(fill in the blank)*.

Now, go back and see what it would take to survive that. No judgments. Don't diminish your particular struggle. Use it as a way into your mind and the many thoughts that create your belief systems. How good are you at surrender? Letting go? Notice how you respond when plans change. When people change. When the weather gets in your way. When you make a mistake. Break something. When you are disappointed. Or when you do the disappointing.

When I began teaching yoga again after a twenty-year hiatus, I thought I needed a balance to the solitariness of writing a book. Some months into my teaching, I realized I was teaching the yoga of loss: with each exhalation, with each position, with each admonition to focus the mind instead of letting it wander, I noticed how the ancient science of yoga teaches us to surrender. We are encouraged to surrender the tight hold we have on our bodies, our breath, and our minds. We are encouraged to let go of the need to be in charge, to hold on, to direct the show. The more we try to make things happen the way we want, the less likely we are to get our way. To ride the horse in the direction it's going is sometimes the greatest teaching.

But how do we trust our inner wisdom if we have not spent time struggling with it, listening to it, being taught by it? The time to seek our inner teacher is not in the face of disaster; it is in the everyday practice of life and loss. As one of the Chassidic masters reminds us: "While a tree with strong roots can withstand a harsh storm, it can hardly hope to grow them once the storm is on the horizon."

Be loss searching for grief.

Bearing the Burden

Only he who suffers can be
the guide and healer of the suffering.

THOMAS MANN

WHAT ARE WE ASKING when we ask someone to please "bear" with us? Are we only asking them to "put up" with us, to follow along even though it probably won't be clear where we are going? By delving into another layer of meaning, I wonder if in asking you to "bear" with me, I am also asking you to "carry" with me as in "to bear a burden." Will you help me carry this for a while? Would you bear this burden with me? Going still deeper, "to bear" also means to give birth, as in: she bore three sons. She carried those babies—a burden of sorts—and at an appointed moment the burden was put down when she "bore" (birthed) them.

The words "grieve" and "grief" come from a French word meaning "to bear a heavy burden." When we grieve with someone or when we grieve for ourselves we bear the burden of sorrow. When we bear a burden together we may help each other to carry the pain of loss and we may even help ourselves to carry what has been lost to us so that, perhaps one day, out of that process, we will give birth to something new.

I recently had a dramatic healing experience relative to my (personal) grief. I was sharing a healing with my friends Ben and Marsha Swirsky and their daughter Shari. You might say the Swirsky family and I set out on this trail together nine years ago when Joel Swirsky, two weeks shy of his nineteenth birthday, died in a car accident. They came to me to share their pain. Not knowing what they were asking, not knowing what I was agreeing to, we decided to bear their grief together. We would go on to carry this grief as equals because I also carried loss (the loss of my relationship to my family) at the center of my soul.

It was Marsha who ultimately convinced me that more of us need to know how to make grief a familiar part of the family into which we are born; more of us need to know that grief need not be exclusively tragic, morbid, and dark. Sometimes it just is. How can we touch the feeling of allowing our grief to simply be? How can we learn to be so honest in the face of our loss that we need not make more of it and not make less of it than it is at any given moment?

Over time, the Swirsky family and I labored together. Eight years after losing her brother, Shari invited me to share her labor as she gave birth to her own child, Jakob Joel. In an ancient initiation attended by her chosen ones, in a "water nest" she had designed, she bore her son. Sharing Shari's labor allowed me to heal parts of my grief "labor" and to share in the healing of her family's grief.

This experience taught me in a very real way the meaning behind the Eastern philosophy that unites creation and destruction in the Hindu Lord Shiva. Shiva, who represents the Hindu deity of destruction and creation, teaches us that every act of creation "bears" within it an act of destruction and every act of destruction "bears" within it an act of creation. The peach rots in order for the peach pit to grow into a tree. The forest grows more green after a fire. Birth and death follow each other. Always and all ways. Endlessly. As day follows night. As spring follows winter. The poet Rabindranath Tagore writes: "Death is not putting out the light. It is extinguishing the lamp because the dawn has come."

To heal, to become whole, asks that we too embody—literally take into our body—the acts of creation that follow death and destruction. According to the Kabbalah, the Jewish mystical tradition, a life does not truly begin until after a person dies. How can that be? Because it is the presence that we continue to have after we are no longer present that acknowledges the power of our being. Our deeds, our actions, are the way we make our presence felt in the world and, to the extent that we continue to influence and impact people's lives after we are dead, we continue to live.

It is also said that after we die, we move further and further away from the body we inhabited and even the world in which we lived. But each time a deed is done in our "memory," each time we serve life in some way, we are called back to the physical plane. We live. To continue to be in the presence of someone we love after death, we need only act positively on their behalf. And, not only are we again with them, but they live for others as well. A hospital wing, a park bench, a scholarship, a painting, an act of charity, a garden, bring the memory out of the past into the present. How often I have appreciated the opportunity to begin a relationship with someone I was meeting posthumously! Someone dared to introduce me to a friend who had died, so that I too could appreciate the wisdom, humor, softness, creativity of one I had not met in life. My husband for example regularly converses with a father-in-law he met six months after his burial.

To bear our grief, to carry our grief, like a pregnancy "to term," means that something is born from it. And that act of birth, heals. In that active process, we become whole. We have dared to carry the act of destruction into an act of creation. We are part of life's mystery. We have been initiated into life's wisdom.

That is why the concept of the word "bereavement" does not initiate us into bearing our grief to term. Bereavement comes from a Latin word meaning "to be robbed." A criminal act has occurred and there is no healing. There is no wholeness. There is a victim whose property has been stolen. There may be revenge and legal recourse but it is a far different path than the path of grieving. With bereavement, I am reminded that nothing on this earth belongs to us—it is all a gift. Even life does not belong to us. A Chassidic story tells us of a Rebbe who would recite a blessing "on meeting his sorrow face to face." He was thanking God for the capacity to recognize his sorrow, the capacity to embrace his sorrow and be embraced by it, and ultimately to bear with his sorrow all the way to that which would be borne from it. Life itself.

The burden of grief is, after all, a call to realize what life is: do we need to have someone or something in a physical form for it to be alive? My son Matt was two and a half years old when I was diagnosed with a malignant tumor. One day as we were driving along in our old Mustang, he asked me: "Mommy, when somebody dies you can't see them anymore, right?" Just as I found myself agreeing with him, I stopped. "No. That's not true," I said, "You can still see them. You can see them in a picture or you can see them in your head." People, places, events don't need to have physical presence to be in our present!

Do we need to have a response to speak to someone? Is it not possible to gratify our need to talk without needing a reply? When I was five years old and my mother returned from sitting shiva for her father, she began a weekly visit with him and her sister Sara who had been dead for many years by then. Was she wacky? On Friday mornings, as the vacuum cleaner drowned out (she assumed) the sound of her voice, she told them everything that was in her heart. Like writing a letter. Sometimes we wait weeks or months for a reply to a letter. Sometimes it never comes. But the catharsis of having written can't be taken from us.

Perhaps the greatest challenge that grief presents is the capacity to be honorable in our grieving. Not to make more of it than it is. And certainly not to make less. To walk that fine line between self-indulgence and denial. To dare to ask the questions that loss, of any kind, brings to us and then to struggle for the honest answer that satisfies our unique soul's journey.

We're all in this alone. Together.

Resources for Transforming
Our Relationship to Loss

part two

The Art of Losing

For whoever has not known himself
has known nothing
but whoever has known himself
has simultaneously achieved knowledge
about the depth of all things.

JESUS

IN OUR CULTURE THE WORST THING you can say about someone is that he is a "loser." But aren't we all losers? Isn't life about chronic loss? The process of life is about endings and beginnings. We are losing all the time. As a matter of a fact, we begin our earthly existence by "losing" time; moment by moment. We usually don't think in these terms but perhaps we should. We breathe in, a beginning; we breathe out, an ending. Life is all about letting go. If we can't "let go" well, then we can't live well. It's all in how we see what we see: We can choose to see it as morbid (defined as "having to do with disease") or we can choose to see it as the rhythm of life. By holding on too tightly we become disconnected from the rhythmic ebb and flow of the world around us. We turn night into day with the flip of a switch and seek to defeat forces of decay and destruction. Loss becomes an affront: this "shouldn't" have happened.

It's our call as to how we live the losing in each moment. Possessions are lost or broken or otherwise disappear. People and relationships change, move on, or die. Pets grow old as we do. Places we loved once are no longer what they were to us. Dreams we once had we might never accomplish or else we change our minds about our desire to realize them.

The ability to "change our mind" is a powerful skill and one we spend a great deal of time with in the face of loss. The power lies in our ability to think about something differently; to think about what loss is and what it means to be a loser. There is an art to living, yes? There is an art to dying, we believe. What about an art to losing, to grieving? We are told, as children, not to be "sore losers" but did anyone teach us how to be "good losers"? Take a deep breath. Reflect on this for a moment. Losing well is freedom—freedom from the pain and confusion and fear attached to loss. We are as surely attached to our pain and fear and confusion around loss as we once were attached to that which we feel we've lost. Perhaps we have substituted our attachment one for the other: the pain for the love. Breathe into the emptiness, breathe into the pain created by loss. Stay for a moment. We love. We give our love to someone or something or someplace. We are attached through that love. And suddenly (or slowly) that object is gone from our sight. Where do we put the love then? We have this love with no place to put it. Grief becomes our experience of not having our love received; of not having anywhere to put our love.

Healing our grief means continuing to love in the face of loss. The face of loss—what we see—is that someone or something is gone. The heart of loss teaches us that nothing—no thing—we have ever known can be lost. What we have known we have taken into ourselves in such a way that it has become part of the very fabric of our being. It is part of who we are and as long as we are alive we have the capacity to continue to love even that which is no longer a part of our daily reality. This means that we will need to "change our minds" about many notions that we have had about loss: That what we can no longer "see" is gone. That what we can no longer touch doesn't continue to live. That if there is no response, the relationship is over.

Close your eyes and see that which you can no longer touch; that which is gone from your presence. Reach inside of you to the feeling of touching, hearing, smelling, being with your experience of what you believed was lost.

Remember.

We are haunted by societal fears that we should not continue to stay connected with what is gone, what is past, what has been lost. There is a pitfall here, a caveat, symbolized by Dickens's Miss Havisham: be wary of that part of us that might want to live in the past. The challenge is to bring the past along with us in such a way that we haven't lost anything. We don't ignore the challenge because of the pitfall. Truth to tell, we could not forget our past if we wanted to. What we choose to leave in the past, we can. What we choose to continue loving, we can. We are being asked to give new form to what was contained in an earlier relationship. Our grief becomes the container for what we feel we have lost and in the process of grieving we come into some new wholeness. We create a way to incorporate, literally to take into our bodies, that which has become formless. Like the caterpillar, we go into a cocoon to a safe place so that the old self can dissolve and a new self can be created.

Like the art of losing, this metamorphosis is not automatic. It does not happen simply in the course of time. Rather, it is a self-conscious act. Grief can be a path to self-realization because in the process of grieving we acknowledge that which we choose not to lose. In the art of losing we can choose who we will be. We break but we break open so that we can include more of life, more of love. We get bigger in order to carry with us what we choose to continue loving.

Breath

If you bring forth what is within you,
what you bring forth will save you.
If you do not bring forth what is within you,
what you do not bring forth will destroy you.

ACTS OF JOHN, GNOSTIC SCRIPTURE

BREATH OPENS US UP. It fills every space that is empty. Breathing is the cornerstone of all pain management, stress management, meditation, and healing disciplines. It is the one activity that is always available to us unaffected by where we are, what we are wearing, or even what we are doing. It is the ultimate universal activity—we all do it in spite of our gender, race, economic or social class. It is free and always available. Perhaps that is why so many of us do not realize the power of the breath to not only focus our attention and clear our thinking but to, literally, change our minds. A friend told me that I didn't need to devote any space in this book to breathing because we all know how to do it. Do we? Do we know how to use this resource as a gift to diminish pain—physical or emotional—to put us in our bodies and minds in a way that strengthens and inspires us?

Inspire: To breathe in. Inspiration. Life begins with our first breath and ends with our last. The first step in learning how to use the many gifts of breath is to pay attention to the in-breath and to the out-breath. First pay attention at the nostrils. Feel the gentle caress as the air enters through the nose and the difference in sensation as you exhale, as the air leaves through the nose. Keep the mouth closed, lightly, not clenching the jaw. Allow the tongue to rest lightly against the back of the teeth.

Just that. No more. Keeping the attention focused at the nostrils as we inhale and exhale, allow the breath, through our attention, to be appreciated. Take the time to slow the breath down. To go deeper. Let the chest expand with the inhalation, fall with the exhalation. Just that. For five minutes or ten or twenty, you have given the mind a rest. You have brought more oxygen, the nourishment needed by every cell in the body, to the system. The exhalation, which eliminates carbon dioxide, cleanses the system. We draw in what we need; we push out what is no longer useful. Human beings are holograms—what we do on the physical level as we inhale and exhale has a concomitant effect on the emotional level.

With the in-breath we draw oxygen into our cells nourishing them. With the in-breath we also draw in what we nourish ourselves with emotionally: love, peace, wisdom, assistance, strength. On the out-breath we release carbon dioxide, a poison gas. We release what is not only no longer useful but what has become perhaps toxic: guilt, shame, blame, fear, anger.

As we look at our habits of thought about loss, as we seek to clarify what our intentions are in our grieving, the breath is the greatest of all allies. To stop the endless parade of unconscious thought; to become adept at witnessing those thoughts so that we can choose the thoughts that will assist us in being who and how we want to be, breath is the ever-present tool for consciousness.

There are hundreds of breathing techniques used by specialists in the field of pain management, stress management, and meditation: lengthening the ratio of the in-breath to the out-breath, speed breathing, hypnotic breathing, exercise breathing. It is not my intention here to teach breathing exercises. It is my intent only to remind us of this power we all have, in the lowering of an eyelid, to stop what we are thinking. What we are feeling. What we are screaming. Just stop. Take a breath. Inhale. By the time you exhale, you have moved. A quarter of a millimeter is movement. You are no longer the victim of your mind. With one breath, you have choice. Take a second. And a third. The old folk wisdom of "count to ten" was the folk wisdom of how ten breaths can open the space for something else to happen. To give you back the reins of the mind.

It is your choice: you can luxuriate in the freedom, the gift, the power of simply breathing. Nothing else to do. No thoughts to wrestle with. Just the air at the tip of the nose going in. Going out. And when you're ready, placing your attention where you choose to place it. Consciously.

Consciousness affects every cell of the body.
Every cell of the body affects consciousness.

PROVERB

Simple Presence – Open Heart

What is this place where thought is useless?
Knowledge cannot fathom it.

YUMEN, ZEN PATRIARCH

We EACH YEARN FOR ONE MOMENT of awe where we can feel connected to the source of life. The moment of a birth, the embrace of unconditional love, the heart of loss each contain such moments. We are essentially changed by these moments, transformed, as we witness birth, embrace love, or feel loss. Yet we protect and defend ourselves from being fully present in these moments because to do so would mean being open not only to life but also to its potential losses. So we construct elaborate defenses against not only loss but against love and other acts of creation. What would it take to stay present and open in the face of love, in the act of creation, or to the challenge of loss?

To stay open we need to have the desire, the intention, the commitment to keep our hearts and minds present. Perhaps what drives the desire to stay present to loss is twofold: both the belief that something, anything, will be revealed to us out of this loss, and the sense that we are pulled into the present by the love we want to continue to have for what we feel is lost. The belief that there is meaning in loss balances the feelings of betrayal with which we are struggling. If we can stay open to the possibility that the loss has happened "for us" and not "to us," then it does not need to be a punishment. We continue to suffer the pain of loss and alongside of it, in addition to the pain, comes something else. What that something else is, is different for each of us in each moment. It is our responsibility in the face of loss to stay present. It is our responsibility to heal the break in the vessel of our being so that we can be available for what comes next.

Belief. Presence. Openness. All of these are ideas in our

minds. Paying attention, observing the parade of thoughts that goes through our minds twenty-four hours a day, is the resource we need in honoring our intention to keep our hearts open and our minds present for the reality of our grief. Ordinarily, we pay no more attention to our thoughts than we pay to the complex digestive or respiratory processes going on in our bodies. Yet thoughts create feelings. Knowing what thoughts go through our minds can move us from being overwhelmed by the pain of what we've lost to trusting that we will weave this loss into the tapestry of our lives. This trust begins to develop by reminding ourselves that we have not "lost" any of our past because it is an integrated part of us and, because it is a part of us, it will continue to be a part of our future. We begin to change our minds about what it "means" to have lost something precious by being an objective observer of the parade of our thoughts and by choosing to have (only) those thoughts that keep us open and present. When we find thoughts that close us down by intensifying our fear or pain, we gently put those thoughts aside. We can say "no" to them sometimes by visualizing a traffic stop sign. Bringing in an image to support our intention to stay open can ease the way. Sometimes a simple image of universal love or peace, a flower, a bird, a sacred place will begin the process.

The third ally in our new relationship to loss is breathing. Simple inhalation and exhalation. By focusing our attention on our breathing, a great deal happens. We change our minds. We move our thoughts intentionally from one object to another. Go ahead. Pay attention to your inhalation. Just notice the breath at the tip of your nose as it enters the body. Slow it down. Deepen it. Notice how it calms you down. When you feel overwhelmed or simply confused in a moment, pay attention to breathing— counting to ten, paying attention to each inhalation, will calm the body/mind reaction. It gives us a moment to regroup, rethink this moment. Where do we want to put our attention? What thoughts do we want to have? What will support us in our intention to stay open, clear, and present? When we feel pain, in our bodies or in our minds, we automatically respond by holding our breath, contracting our muscles, closing down in defense. Our decision to fight against pain, resist it, actually keeps us in pain longer. By thinking ourselves, breathing ourselves, soft around the pain, the pain quiets down.

Intention, objective observation, and breathing are the tools for simple presence in the face of loss. This is as true for those surrounding the one in grief as it is true for the "griever." Over the years I have often been approached by friends, families, and coworkers who fear that they will say or do the "wrong" thing. It is as important for the people around us to stay open and honest about our loss as it is for us. In the moment that we look at someone meeting the challenge of divorce, death, disease, or betrayal as if this is happening to "them" and not to us, we lose our openness, our presence. The gift we bring to each other in these moments is this gift of camaraderie. We don't usually think of camaraderie when we think of grief and loss, we usually think of loneliness, separation, and isolation. But the truth is that what is happening today in my life will also happen, perhaps tomorrow, in your life. Maybe not in exactly the same form, but close enough.

When Bill Cosby's son Ennis was murdered, Mr. Cosby had the "presence" to reach out to those other families who were that day also facing the murder of their children. He was not alone. And when I sit in simple presence with a friend or client or colleague struggling with financial loss or a loss of health, dare I separate myself into thinking this is "her" struggle and not mine?

Some time ago I was invited to speak to a group of bereaved parents. Before I began the seminar a man stood up and asked if I had a child that had died and if I didn't what right did I have to be leading this group? After more than a decade of sitting with families struggling to integrate the death of a child, I was able to honestly say to this man: "When your child dies, my child dies! In sitting with you with an open heart, I sacrifice my innocence, my arrogance, in thinking that I am safer than you are." We are all at risk at all times. The only mistake I can make in being with a friend or family member who is grieving is separating myself from them. The only error is in trying to touch your pain with my mind instead of with my heart. The fear of contagion, the fear of getting too close to grief and "catching it" keeps us isolated.

The wisdom that teaches us that we have all been exposed to loss from the moment of our birth keeps us connected to each other. Say what is in your heart and if there are no words, trust the silence. Do what is in your heart and if there is nothing to do, do nothing with your heart open.

Shadow Work

We are all vulnerable to the unexplored.

TALMUD

COULD ANY OF US WATCHING PETER PAN struggling with his shadow—to find his shadow, to keep his shadow, and, ultimately, to "bind" his shadow to him—have known that the shadow carries powerful psychological implications? We might have noticed that Peter seemed different once his shadow was firmly attached. He was still delightful and charming but slightly subdued and not quite so self-centered and irresponsible. A bit more . . . dare we say, grown up?

Shadow depends upon light whether it be the light of the sun, the light of creation, or the light of love. Try as we might to separate them, we can't. Light and shadow form a unit. Similarly, at an emotional level, what is stored in the shadow is necessary to make ourselves whole. We can't simply tiptoe past it and hope we'll come out all right. Peter Pan, after all, began to die without his shadow!

As Peter could tell us, the shadow is vague, elusive, and hard to pin down. It not only contains parts of us critical to our wholeness (and therefore to our healing), it also contains immense energy. What we don't want to know; what we struggle to avoid, resist, deny, and disown carries a disproportionate amount of force. The unconscious mind, where the shadow lives, is like the iceberg under the surface of the ocean, as opposed to the conscious mind that is the tip (of the iceberg), which we can see. It was what was hidden beneath the surface that sank the unsinkable Titanic in mere minutes.

What is hidden in the shadow looms large, menacing and sinister. When we turn on the light we are often relieved to discover it was an old hat or a coat hastily thrown over the bedpost. Sometimes, when we turn on the light, we are thrilled to find in the shadow something we believed was lost, or worse, stolen.

Hidden in the shadow of loss is the power of the love we continue to carry for the person, place, or moment in time we fear is lost to us. When my dear father died, an event I had been preparing for all my life, an amazing quiet descended. In the emptiness of loss, a calm and peace as I had known only in deep meditation or prayer enveloped me. The voice on the other end of the phone, at 5:20 a.m., quietly told me my father had died. The light of my life had gone out. I waited in the darkness hearing his last words to me: "I've loved you more than life."

Life had not been kind to my dad. Though my brothers and I were raised into lives of relative financial ease, my father was a laborer. He drove a delivery truck for thirty years at night through harsh, bitter winters and hot, miserable summers. He was lonely and ill for all the years of his retirement. Yes, his love for me had been greater than his love for life and, for me, he was everything. He was mother, father, sister, brother, grandfather, the whole family. Constant and unconditional in his love, I needed him like air or water. When he asked me if I was ready for him to die, I assured him that I was OK. My heart beat wildly. What was I saying? Then I remembered, I wanted to help him on his way. Go in peace.

Six weeks later he died. As I prepared myself to fly to New York for his funeral and then to Philadelphia to sit shiva, I continued to be surrounded by this otherworldly quiet. It was as if I were waiting for something. And then something came and landed in that open hole in my heart that had, for forty-four years, contained my father. All the love, respect, appreciation, and admiration that I had given to this remarkable man—this simple, ordinary man—started coming back to me. As I flew across the sky in a jumbo jet, imagining our paths might be crossing (!), it was as if his emotional bank accounts were being emptied. He no longer needed anything. All of the deposits we had made, plus interest, were being delivered to me as his beneficiary. All the love, honor, and respect I had given to him were coming back to me. I had never thought or read or heard such a thought. Yet, here it was, happening to me, filling me up in that place that would have otherwise been forever filled with the pain of loss.

That was the beginning of my apprenticeship to the shadow of grief and loss. That experience, which has continued to shape me in the face of many subsequent losses, taught me that we need to stay open and present in the face of grief and allow the emptiness to be. If we fill it with our pain, there won't be room for anything else. Yes, the pain is there. The loss is real. Yet, there is the possibility of something else, there is the nascent possibility of receiving back everything we have invested in that friendship, love, job, marriage, home, or child.

I learned that the pain of grief is also not having a place to put the love, the creativity, the passion we had given to our beloved. Hidden in the shadow of loss is the power, the sheer physical energy, to create something out of that love. The Talmud tells us that a person's life does not begin until after they die! How can that be? Because, during our lifetime, the impact we have on life is a result of our physical presence. But after we die, if our existence continues to be felt, we have attained eternal life!

When Stacey Levitt, an eighteen-year-old poet, was killed by a car as she was out jogging one evening, her family was struck senseless. Beloved by father, mother, sisters, they took up Stacey's pen. Her family wrote poetry for her, to her, and eventually published her poetry. In one of her own poems, Stacey shared the following:

Encounter with Death

I saw death the other day.
I had a meeting with it at 9:00,
at its office downtown.
There were a few questions I needed to ask.
I was expecting to see a dark shadow
with sharp teeth and claws.
But,
when I got there I was met by a kind,
old woman.
She smiled at me
and brought me to her office.
It was like she could read my thoughts
because right away she said,
So, you want to know about 'The other side.'
Yes, I replied, please tell me about it.
I listened eagerly.
Well it's not what it seems,
as you've probably already noticed,
she said calmly.
Death is not evil with devils,
nor kind with angels.
It is simply me
taking you in
so you can fight through another life
much like you do now.
So I smiled and said,
Death really isn't so bad after all.
So what if I die?
Everyone's greatest fear is death,
but not for me anymore.

Now I can live my life free,
free from the fear of death.
I guess coming face to face
with your fear
and talking it out
really does pay off.
As I got up to leave, I said,
Thank you, Mrs. Death,
and I'm sorry, but I can't stay
any longer.
I now have an appointment
with guilt.

Stacey was twelve years old when she wrote this poem. Was she prescient? Did she have a foreshadowing of her early death? The fact that we can participate in Stacey's life today through her poetry tells us that her parents dared to go into the darkness of their loss and bring out the gold of Stacey's life! Her life outlives her. In laboring to bring forth Stacey's poetry, her family transforms their darkness into light and participates in healing not only themselves but the whole world too.

Grieving can be one of the most difficult and rewarding experiences we will ever encounter. Loss challenges all of our fiercely held beliefs that if we just don't think about "it," "it" won't happen. The inevitable, perhaps even anticipated, result is that when "it" (the unthinkable) does happen, we give ourselves and each other permission to collapse in the face of our disbelief. In "falling apart," we separate from each other. Together, we can acknowledge the reality that there are forces operating beyond our control. Together, we honor the vulnerability every single one of us carries whether we are poor or rich, beautiful or hideous, charming or misfits. Together, we all meet in a place called grief. And that grief, honestly engaged, will connect us all to the very nature of life. Life is loss and loss is life's shadow.

When we shine light in the shadows, the shadows disappear and we can see what has been lurking there: our anger, covering our fear of chaos and the unknown; our laziness, unwilling to be held accountable for our behavior; our self-indulgence that wants to hold on to the way it was "supposed to be." Even those parts of us that are promiscuous in our suffering and loss insist: "I earned this misery and no one is going to take it away."

From the shadows of the unconscious, the collapse around grief is what psychologists would call a "secondary gain." We are allowed and even expected to be out of control; we can indulge our rages and emotional excesses. We don't have to "behave." Our emotions have carte blanche and there are no expectations we have to meet. The danger, however, in keeping to the shadow, is the danger of falling too far into any one of those trapdoors. The danger is that to prove our love we will respond to the expectations others have of us; if we are not "crazed" with grief, did we not love? So we wind up feeding the shadow instead of nourishing ourselves. The pain itself validates us. Our suffering makes loss a tragedy and we are seduced by the drama of that tragedy as individuals and as a culture. Anything that perpetuates that drama—anger, blame, guilt—is embraced. What we do not allow ourselves to embrace is the possibility that if we are not so singularly focused on the tragedies of loss, we might stumble onto the teaching, the wisdom, the initiation into the mystery of life that loss can be.

Einstein offered up one of the keys to that mystery by teaching us that energy can never be destroyed. It just changes form. Since every single thing on the face of this earth is some kind of energy nothing can ever ultimately be destroyed. Perhaps the challenge to the shadow of grief might be to stand in the face of the onslaught of what could be overwhelming forces of destruction and find the forces of creation. What new form has this energy taken? How can I now interact with him, her, it? The greatest challenge to our grief might be to re-create ourselves in the face of the death of who we no longer are.

Imagine

The only difference between stumbling blocks
and stepping stones is how we use them.

SUSAN SALISBURY RICHARDS

CARL JUNG, THE RENOWNED PSYCHOLOGIST, said that healing lives in the realm of the imaginal. Where exactly is "the realm of the imaginal"? The imaginal lives in what we see with our imagination, the vision of the mind's eye. Most of us have grown up in a culture where the imagination has been grossly underrated. If you want to invalidate a friend's feelings you tell them that what they are feeling is "just their imagination," or respond with, "it's all in your mind" to someone's fears. But our minds are all we've got. The imagination lets a blind person see; the imagination is where dreams are born; the imagination is where healing begins. Healing, the act of remembering ourselves back into wholeness after we've been dismembered, begins as a thought, as an idea, as a picture we have in our minds.

What are the pictures we have associated with loss? A void. An abyss. A black hole. These are images I have heard described at least a thousand times. When I began to walk with others in grief, we had to create new images for grief and loss. We sought images that would contain the process of grieving with honor; that would not diminish it or disrespect it. One of the first images that presented itself was of grief as a landscape, as a country we are visiting: sometimes we are visiting voluntarily and sometimes we are cast up on its shores, strangers in a strange land. We need to learn its customs, its language, and its pathways.

Grief is the ground we walk on. Can we imagine it green instead of black? The Chinese *Book of Changes* says that the forest grows more green after a fire. Can we hold that image? Yes, there are parts of us that yell and scream at what seems to be our feeble attempts to make this horrible loss acceptable. But can we even allow ourselves the thought, the image, the possibility of new growth? Rachel Naomi Remen, a physician and author, says that the void created by a loss can be seen as an unopened present. Our minds rail: "This? A gift? It's a horror!" Yes. But is it possible to consider it might also contain something else?

My friends tease me at my consummate capacity to rationalize everything. My answer to that is that we are supposedly rational beings. Why not use our evolutionary superiority? We do not have the power, I believe, to change what has happened. But we do have the power to change how we think and how we see and what we imagine about what has happened. This is not a form of denial. Healing in the realm of the imaginal means looking at the images we have in our minds; listening to the thoughts with which we are obsessed; hearing the words that are coming out of our mouths; and making a conscious decision to have thoughts and images, and speak words that bring us back into wholeness.

When we talk about grief as a landscape, I have always imagined the land of Narnia in C. S. Lewis's *The Chronicles of Narnia*. In the book's first volume, *The Lion, The Witch and The Wardrobe*, Lisa hides in an old wardrobe in a long-abandoned room in her uncle's house. As she waits for one of her brothers or sisters to find her, she burrows farther and farther back into the dark closet. Suddenly, she becomes aware of leaves and twigs beneath her feet. The ground is frozen, there is a street lamp and a mythic creature. Thus begins an incredible journey. In Narnia there are warm and comfortable places as well as cold and forbidding ones. People are not uniformly good or uniformly bad: it is an absolutely altered reality. Just like grief. Not absolutely bad. Not absolutely good. Sometimes the way is clear and sometimes it is fraught with peril.

Just like grief. An enchanted though not necessarily enchanting image.

The landscape of grief is also reminiscent of Alice falling down the rabbit hole. One moment she is dozing in the garden and the next moment falling, falling, falling into a world where nothing is right. Who is she? What is she? Where is she? Eventually, after many trials and tribulations, Alice wakes up. But she will never look at things quite the same way again. Grief is like this, too.

In the book *Paula,* author Isabel Allende tells how she sat at the bedside of her daughter Paula, who lay for a year in a coma before she died. Isabel's mother says to her daughter: "You are going through a long dark tunnel but you must believe that there is a light at the end of it. You must believe it because I tell you so. You will come out the other side." When you come out the other side of grief who will you be? What will you be? It all rests in your mind, in your willingness to imagine it.

Can you imagine healing from loss in such a way that the healing itself gives life to what was lost? So that there is no loss, there is only change.

The parade of thoughts going through our minds and the stream of words coming out of our mouths nourish our imagination. If our thoughts and words derive from only one of the basic food groups, we will be malnourished. If we feed ourselves only thoughts of devastation and pain and suffering without opening to the breathing spaces in between, we will be malnourished.

It takes effort and awareness to balance our diets. We must shop for the foods we need and take the time to prepare a proper meal. Our thoughts are the preparation for the meal that our words become. We are nourished or starved by the thoughts we allow into our minds and the words that come out of our mouths.

Knowing full well that every once in a while, we all need junk food, we need to be compassionate with those times when we collapse without resource; when we are exhausted from the effort of simple presence; when we allow ourselves to fall apart—but not so far apart that we lose sight of our responsibility to our wholeness.

Instead of focusing our attention on the personal pronoun of "why me?" ask the bigger question "why?" In asking for the teaching, we pray for the wisdom, courage, and strength to be with what is instead of wishing for what isn't. In loss we are asked to learn how to be in a relationship with an unseen being. We have to open our minds to our imagination and then want the imaginal relationship to develop. When someone asked an elderly friend of mine why she still talked to her husband since his death, she replied: "I've been talkin' to Herbie for fifty-seven years. He'd be mad at me if I stopped talkin' just because he died!" In another instance, a client told me how after his mom died, he would automatically reach for the phone for their daily call. "Why stop?" he asked himself as he imagined the speed-dial getting her number. Can you imagine that?

Sometimes we want to sit down and write a letter to someone or something we are missing. Writing letters—letters that we might just write and mail in our imagination or literally write and mail to some "dead letter" department—can be an exercise in not only creativity but in healing the empty places in our lives, especially if we allow ourselves to imagine what response we might get from the addressee!

Special days—birthdays, anniversaries, holidays—cry out to us for attention. One year, after my father's death, I actually bought him a Father's Day card and now, each year on that day, I put it out on my desk. It's still Father's Day and he's still my dad, after all. My friend Marsha called me one day to say she had seen a beautiful book on sports heroes that her deceased son Joel would have loved and that she had bought it for him, for herself, and ultimately to share with her new son-in-law. I was inspired by her willingness to go past the empty place where Joel "isn't" to the place where Joel still "is." Not just out there someplace, but right in Marsha's life and in the lives of all who know Joel.

Last year on the date of my dad's birthday I decided to take him out for a walk with me around town. I had moved to San Clemente shortly before his death and he never got to know this beautiful little town. I took him to all my favorite "haunts"—to have a bowl of soup at my little luncheon spot, to "meet" my favorite people. It seemed that I had a perfect Dad story to share with each person I ran into that day and I was aware of how happy everyone was to be with me and my unseen dad. Often they had a story to share or questions to ask. The day was a gift I gave myself.

One morning I received a call from a woman whose husband had died almost a year before. She was a counselor and was starting a support group for widows. What about sexual feelings? she asked. She was not yet ready to go out and engage with a new man, but nonetheless she was longing to be held. As we talked about her sense of loss each morning waking up alone and not feeling her husband's embrace, she began to consider what it might be like to imagine her husband's physical presence and to feel him holding her in loving embrace. By using her sense memories (touch, smell, taste), could she derive some measure of comfort? When feeling his absence, could she then imagine his presence? Some weeks later, a cryptic message was left on my answering machine: "It's working."

Sometimes we need a "centering image" that we can call on whenever we are feeling vulnerable to the forces of loss. A centering image is a picture we can pull up on our mental screen that immediately softens our hearts and minds and makes us smile. This image can be the memory of a moment in time or a place you have visited. It can be a religious symbol that brings with it a feeling of serenity or the face of a beloved. A centering image is an image that melts the hardness around the pain and brings with it a feeling of peace. Such an image brings us back to our emotional center; a place of balance where we can recharge our batteries by connecting to some source. When we encounter other images, images that disturb and disrupt our sense of wholeness, we can quietly replace those with a healing image. This is what Jung meant when he said that healing lives in the imaginal. Healing lives in the images with which we choose to live.

Surrender

When old words die out on the tongue,
new melodies spring forth from the heart.

RABINDRANATH TAGORE

FERTILE GROUND THAT PRODUCES HEALTHY GROWTH does so because it has been properly tended in the early cycles of the planting season. The ground of our own being likewise needs to be prepared in such a way that we can learn and grow through the losses in our lives. If the ground we are seeking to plant has not had its soil cleared of rocks and stones; if the soil has not been turned over; if we do not enrich the land with nutrients; then our field won't yield its best crop.

Our rush to judgment, our addiction to comparisons, and our obsession with understanding might be conditions of thinking that will not yield fertile soil for growth. To learn, we need an open and receptive mind. We need a field that has been cleared of the stones and rocks of (moralizing) judgments. "Let he who is without sin cast the first stone." When we judge a person or an event, when we cast our stones in judgment, we destroy the crop before it has even been planted. When we look at any experience of loss as if it shouldn't have happened, as if it could have been avoided, or as if it is a travesty of divine justice, we harden our minds and our hearts. We become stony and hard-hearted; adjectives that conjure up a path that is difficult to walk much less a field that will be possible to till.

If we compound our rush to judgment with an obsessive need to understand, we make it almost impossible to stay open to plant the seeds within the loss. Sometimes we can't understand an event, not now and not ever. Sometimes, by staying present and open, understanding eventually comes. Understanding or "standing under" an experience gives us a particular perspective. We are not above it or bigger than the event. We are not alongside of it or equal to it. We are under it, beneath it. Perhaps "understanding" is telling us that learning comes when we surrender. Surrender our need. Surrender our judgments, surrender our habit of comparing, and surrender our need to understand.

Comparing losses, saying that the grief experienced by a woman rejected from medical school is less than the grief of a man newly diagnosed with cancer doesn't serve anyone. The young woman is deprived of her honest experience of loss and the man, by becoming the standard through which other grief is judged, finds himself isolated and robbed of his personal process. Comparisons separate us into inviolate containers of grief. When we compare losses, we separate out those worthy of mourning from those not worthy of mourning. We are isolated from each other in our comparative positions and are not able to draw from our common well of grief.

There is no competition, no elite cadre, on the field of mourners. Too often I have sat with the wounded. Either they were judged lacking, if their loss didn't warrant their grief, or they were the ones who won the sweepstakes. Their loss was agreed to be "the worst." Is this supposed to be a comfort? I remember sitting in my office as a woman whose son had died in a car accident left and a man who had been betrayed by a family member into near bankruptcy came in. The man, out of his mind with pain and fear, said: "It would be easier if my son had died . . . at least then I could grieve!"

Our job is not to sit in horrified judgment, admonishing him for his words anymore than it is our job to tell the little girl whose dog has been hit by a car that her grief is not as bad as the little boy's with crippling arthritis. The grief we each meet and carry in the moment of loss has its own integrity that ought not to be compromised by judgment, comparison, or the need to understand. It is what it is. What it will become is a function of the condition of the soil in which it has been planted. We are not asked to judge, compare, or understand grief. We are only asked to be willing to hold it in our hearts.

There are pains that cannot be contained in the mind—
only in the heart.

STEPHEN LEVINE

State of Witness

A hole is nothing at all, but you can break your neck in it.

AUSTIN O'MALLEY

INTENTION IS THE ABILITY to decide what it is we want to achieve and then setting out to achieve that goal. We use the power of intention in business, politics, and education. Can we use it in healing our pain?

When we set our intention to heal, we make a one hundred percent commitment to take responsibility for our thoughts. We don't "try" to listen to our thoughts, or "hope" to listen to our thoughts, or "wish" to listen to our thoughts, we just do it. Even when we're not succeeding we're still engaging the process. Just not successfully in the moment. How can we then choose those thoughts that will keep us open to the unlayering of our experiences and to the transformation that is at the core? By "setting our intention."

There is a state of consciousness we call the witness state. In the witness state, or objective consciousness, we begin to listen to the parade of our thoughts. We set our intent. We watch the thoughts go by as if we were watching a parade. We don't exercise critical judgment about what we are thinking; we simply become adept at watching our thoughts. We are eavesdropping on the conversation going on in our minds. After a while we begin to recognize certain thoughts that promote a feeling of well-being as well as others that torque us and intensify feelings of anguish. Do we want the anguish? Sometimes the answer is yes. Can we protect ourselves from getting lost in the anguish? Can we provide a life preserver to get us out before we drown? What does choosing anguish do for helping us achieve our intention?

Two and a half years after the death of my father, my husband

and I took a trip to Hawaii. It was my first time visiting the island. As we landed, I felt a wave of father-loss wash over me such as I had not yet felt. All I could feel was how gone my dad was. I was shocked by the intensity and the unexpectedness of these feelings. I told Bill immediately and we took a walk outside the terminal. In the warm gentle rain it was easy to weep, to be present for what I was honestly feeling. It passed through me in a very brief time. No more, and no less.

What does it take to be vigilant in moments of loss, so that we are not seduced by our own drama, our own tears? One of the dangers in grieving is the possibility of contamination. We contaminate the honesty of a moment's loss with any other loss that we have not yet integrated or acknowledged. When one grief bleeds into another we can become promiscuous in our grieving. We get lost in an ocean of grief instead of negotiating the inlet of one specific loss.

The pain of loss can be overwhelming. When we are in pain, everything in us wants to close down. In the process we often shut out precisely what we need. We lock ourselves inside with the pain as if an intruder has entered our home and, in locking the doors and barring the windows, we lock ourselves inside with the enemy. But is pain "the enemy" or is it there to remind us that we are in some kind of danger? Pain is a biofeedback mechanism. It is a gift of evolution that lets us know something is wrong and we need to find out what it is. Accurately. If we identify the pain in our side as a result of a bruise and it is really a ruptured appendix, we are in trouble!

To penetrate the origins of our pain in relation to loss takes a great deal of attention and intention. We don't want to simply get rid of the pain through physical or emotional anesthetics until we have come face to face with what it needs to tell us. By honoring the presence of pain, by acknowledging the appropriateness of the pain, by being willing to face the pain, we pay attention to it in a way that begins to allow us to have a relationship with it. "What?" you ask, "have a relationship with pain?" Crazy as it might sound, pain is one path to the sacred.

The sacred is that which is holy. To be holy is to be whole. Pain and love are not two sides of the same coin, they are one coin. To love is to risk pain, to invite pain into our lives. The word "passion" comes from the Latin "to suffer." When we are most passionate, whether with a person or an idea, we suffer the loss of ourselves in another. And when that other leaves us, we are bereft.

The alternative to choosing anguish is to allow ourselves to stay open to the pain that, in effect, honors the love. There is a difference between staying open to the pain and collapsing in the pain. That is why we must pay attention to ourselves and our intention. What do we intend to do with this pain? How will we host this loss? It is up to us whether we lose ourselves in the loss or whether we use the loss as a path to deeper wisdom. If the very essence of life is loss, then loss takes us to life's essence. The first half of a sentence is lost even as we are saying the second half. Each minute, as it goes by, is lost. Cells are dying as we speak. The Buddhist teacher, Thich Nhat Hanh, tells us that the rose is on its way to becoming garbage and the garbage is on its way to becoming a rose.

Ignorance is not bliss! What we don't know we are thinking can hurt us. The first step in healing is paying attention to what pulls us to one side or another. In those moments when we are alone and not actively engaged—perhaps as we travel from one destination to another, as we wait in line at the bank or on hold on the telephone or in quiet contemplation at the beach or in the woods or at home—practice listening to the thoughts parading through your mind. Notice the ones that are healing, supportive. Notice those that create pain, doubt, and fear. Gently pluck the thoughts that are not going to take you where you want to go. Pluck the thoughts out as if they were weeds in your garden. Pluck them out, without judgment, anger, or resentment because they don't serve you and because it is your intention to heal.

For instance, if I find myself thinking that I will never see my father again and I notice a profound sadness, I pay attention to what comes next. If I continue to deepen into the loss in such a way that I suffer more and more deeply, I take a deep breath. I acknowledge the absence that his death brings to me. But I also acknowledge the many ways in which I continue to feel him, hear him, see him. In one such moment, I come to realize that although my father has been dead for four years my love for him has continued to grow in that time. Each day of my life the love I have for my father has gotten bigger, unimpeded by his physical absence. I love that thought! No one had ever told me that "growing" the love we have for someone is not dependent upon their being physically alive. I could not have arrived at that thought if I had continued spiraling down deeper and deeper into my suffering at his absence. My intention is to honor his presence not his absence.

By paying attention to our intention we commit to being present with our hearts open, allowing the free movement of feelings. We resist being attached to one feeling or resistant to another. Let them come and go. Grieving asks that we be fully present in our thoughts and then to choose, responsibly, those thoughts that honor the relationship for which we grieve.

Healing the Mystical Body of Loss

part three

The Spiral Dance

To everything there is a season,
and a time to every purpose under heaven.

ECCLESIASTES 3:1

CHRISTIANITY OFFERS US A TEACHING on the art of forgiveness. Tibetan Buddhism offers us a teaching on the art of dying. Judaism offers a teaching on the art of grieving. The spirit in the world today as we enter the third millennium feels to be one of sharing powerful traditions and healing arts contained within each culture. The notion of one world, one people is an idea that allows us to pick and choose among the strengths that we each have.

As a lifelong student of the world's spiritual and religious traditions and a devoted student of Tibetan Buddhism in particular, I remember the moment a friend told me that the Dalai Lama asked to meet with a group of Rabbis. Why? Because, he said, the Jews have a long history of maintaining the strength of their tribe even in the Diaspora, even in exile. And he, the Dalai Lama, was now the spiritual leader of a tribe in exile. It might have been in that moment where I saw Buddhism and Judaism come together and touch each other that I also saw the place where the art of dying contained in Tibetan Buddhism would be met by the art of grieving in Judaism.

Judaism has an interesting conception of time. Rather than viewing time as a linear progression, a sequence of successive moments, Jewish teachings speak of cycles of time. As each new day begins, the cycle of creation begins anew. The Hebrew word for year, "shana," alludes to this concept because it also means "repetition." Each year, each day, each moment is both new and old; it contains both the known as well as the unknown.

Out of this wisdom comes a map for our journey into the landscape of grief that is nothing if not a journey into the unknown. The known is carried by that which we grieve and the unknown is that territory marked by living without it. As we begin the first year of our grief, we enter planetary time—the first day as the earth revolves around its own axis; the first month as the moon revolves around the earth; and the first year as the earth revolves around the sun. Each of these cycles beckon to our fearful selves as we ask the question: How can I face the next minute, the next hour much less the rest of my life without my beloved?

In my work both with my own grief and with those who have shared their journey into grief with me, I have been amazed over and over again at the healing wisdom of accounting for these cycles in our revolution through grief. The journey begins with a year of "firsts." There is the first Monday, the first July 4th, the first Christmas, the first New Year's, or family gathering . . . the first snowfall, the first trip to the beach, the first birthday. Abraham Heschel, the great twentieth century biblical scholar writes, "There is a realm of time where the goal is not to have but to be, not to own but to give, not to control but to share, not to subdue but to be in accord."

How can we be in "accord" with these cycles or rhythms of grief? Elisabeth Kübler-Ross, the well-known author of *On Death and Dying*, first noted the five distinct stages we go through as we face the reality of death: denial, depression, anger, bargaining, and acceptance. These phases are played out whether we are dealing with the passing of a beloved or facing our own death. We will most likely encounter them in other difficult situations not related to death as well.

In the highly ritualized framework Judaism offers us to help contain and heal our grief, these cycles of time are clearly acknowledged. Social amenities, professional commitments, and even religious obligations are canceled in recognition of the mourner's troubled mind. We are literally "out of circulation" for the week following the burial of a family member. We don't leave the house. Our community comes to us to mourn, to pray, and to feed us. It is customary to cover the mirrors in a house of mourning so that we are neither seduced into caring for our vanity nor terrified by the face of our grief.

As we move from the denial of the first day into the depression of the first week, we are at least physically safe in a home environment surrounded and cared for by our family and community.

After the shiva week, we venture forth from our homes. We begin to come out of denial and depression often to find anger. Anger at whomever or whatever visited this suffering upon us and our loved ones. During that first month, though we return to work and begin to honor again basic obligations, we may still wear some outer sign of our grief like the clothing torn at the gravesite or the unshorn hair and beard for male mourners.

Once we enter the cycle of the first year we find ourselves spiraling through all of these earlier stages—denial, depression, anger—and into a fourth stage: bargaining. How can I make it? What will it take for me to survive this? I'll change jobs; I'll help others in this situation; I'll not be bothered by what seemed so important before this loss and now seems trivial. During this year we do not fully rejoin our social lives. We might still find parties and merriment, music and lighthearted entertainments difficult to bear. And that is as it should be! The very foundation of our lives, our beliefs, has been shaken. Can we not give ourselves over to a full cycle of time—a year—to reconstitute ourselves?

After the year is over, we move into a cycle that Kübler-Ross calls acceptance. Judaism provides a ritual of remembrance that helps us to accept. This ritual not only embraces the anniversary of the death but also includes a moment during each holy day—Tabernacles, Passover, Pentecost and The Day of Atonement—where we light a candle, say a prayer, and honor the soul of our loss.

Judaism marks "anniversary grief." Often thought to be like a monster lurking around a dark corner waiting to pounce, this aspect of grief catches us sometimes unsuspectingly and sometimes with dreaded expectation. Yizkor, the prayer recited four times a year in synagogues throughout the world, is a prayer of "remembering." The word comes from the root word in Hebrew "Lizkor," to remember. What wisdom to place at the center of our festivities a prayer of remembering, so that we do not find ourselves in the midst of celebration without a vessel, without a container, for our grief. If the art of grieving is to be in accord with (the spirit of) time, then we must take the time to honor our grief over and over and over again.

Although I have seen a psychological model for mourners used by contemporary grief therapists that consists of four stages (shock, denial, anger, alienation) I have always noticed the synchronicity of the rhythms of grieving with those of death and dying. After all, the mourner has died, too! If we line up Kübler-Ross's stages with the Jewish model we have:

Denial—Day

Depression—Week

Anger—Month

Bargaining—Year

Acceptance—Ongoing

Of course we know that these emotional stages are not sequential, it is more like a spiral. We keep coming back to our disbelief, our anger, our depression, our acceptance, over and over again. But each time we are a little bit different, a little bit changed by the interval, and so we have a spiral movement. It is what some call the spiral dance of life bringing us back over and over again to those people, places, memories, and ideas that form us.

This framework that the calendar offers to us in our grief does not just speak to the loss of a family member. Any loss that is the loss of a "familiar" will ebb and flow and ask for healing or, at least, acknowledgment within these cycles of time.

Once, in a telephone conversation, I met a young woman who had recently been diagnosed with multiple sclerosis (MS). As her three young children played in the background, Susie spoke in whispered sentences. Her fear was palpable across three thousand miles of telephone wires. "How long ago were you diagnosed?" I asked. "Three days," she told me. "You need to sit shiva," I said, explaining that shiva is the seven-day period after the burial of a family member, in this case Susie's MS-free body. Take the time to go inside, literally if possible, I urged her. Put aside all ordinary concerns as much as possible and sink into this place. Be safe and protected by your family and friends and home. "Oh my God," she gasped. "That's why I haven't wanted to go outside! That's why I just want to stay inside with my friends, my family, with people I love and trust."

Yes. Our instincts are often more in accord with the needs of our grieving than are our cultural commands. Grief ultimately connects us to the rhythms of life itself as day follows night and light comes again after the darkness of loss.

Ritual of Remembering

Give sorrow words.
The grief that does not speak
whispers the o'erfraught heart and bids it break.

MACBETH

WHILE LIVING IN TUCSON, I was invited to hear Kote Lotah, a Choumash shaman, share his views of medicine with students at the University of Arizona Medical School. Kote is one of those people you trust instinctively, believing he is speaking the truth. As the students questioned him about specific medical problems, he began to focus on women's health issues. He spoke of the effect on a woman's aura, her energy field, each time she becomes pregnant. Whether the pregnancy results in a birth or not, he said that her auric field is pierced by the entry and exit of the potential fetus. Having just come from my gynecologist who recommended that I have a hysterectomy, I asked if Kote would perform a healing ritual for me. Later that night he did. Then I knew his wisdom was true.

Each time someone or something of importance enters our lives, our physical, emotional, mental, and spiritual fields are pierced. And each time we experience a loss, our "field" is similarly pierced. Loss not only pierces our aura but it dismembers us. The degree to which we were attached (to what we now experience as gone) is the degree to which we are dismembered. So many mothers whose children have died would speak to me of the pain they would feel, literally, in their wombs. But it is not only the death of a child or a beloved that causes this implosion; it is the loss of any relationship that we feel we need to be whole, to survive. It may be a lover, a home, a job, a pet. In losing the "relation" it is as if we have lost the integrity of our system. A piercing of our energy field has taken place and caused the system to dismember.

Remembering is an essential ingredient in mourning. By saying Yizkor, the "remembering" prayer, our teachers of long ago understood that there would be times that our hearts and minds would naturally turn to our loss. Certainly the anniversary date is forever struck in our memories but times of celebration and festive occasions also bring us face to face with the challenge of commingling our joy with our sorrow. So that we don't need to fear that we will forget, we make a ritual of remembering.

There is a custom in the synagogue that anyone not saying Yizkor is asked to leave until the prayer is complete. As a child, I thought it was to protect me from the sadness and pain of grief. The first time I said Yizkor for my father, I learned the ritual was not to protect the ones leaving the temple but to protect the sanctity and the intimacy of the sacred space for those remaining. Yizkor, an opportunity to be with the purity of remembering, is heightened by being in the company of others who are doing the same.

When I hear about the struggles faced by those in grief as holidays, birthdays, weddings loom on the horizon and the paralysis brought on by the thought of how to meet joy in the face of grief, I remind myself that there are cycles to our grieving and cycles to our remembering. In the first year of mourning we don't want to participate fully in celebrations. Our hearts and minds, our bodies and spirits rail at the very idea. We withdraw from casual socializing and merrymaking. Even our ears sometimes resist the very music that floats our way! All of these are suggestions that our worlds have not been shattered.

When we are involved with the process of remembering we are learning how to put ourselves, our "members," back together. We are reconfiguring ourselves in such a way that includes what is no longer physically present in our lives. With thought and intention and time, we begin to manage what seemed impossible at the beginning. We are weaving this loss into the tapestry of our very being as we discover the relationship is not lost. The "other" is now no longer separate from us but eternally part of our physical being. The pain in the womb a mother feels when her child dies is perhaps the part of her laboring to reconceive her child in the face of death. To bear her child back into life!

When my friend Sydelle died, I realized she was with me so much more often than when she was alive. We didn't need to wait to see each other or connect on the phone, she was simply there in the moment I would think of her. That was many years ago and I have learned that to be true through many subsequent losses. And not only of people but of moments and feelings and sacred places. It is my responsibility, it is the responsibility of grief, to remember myself in such a way that I include what I don't choose to lose. I lose something over and over again when I don't remember that, as long as I live, "it" is a part of me and therefore "it" lives too. Not as "it" did before but then I, too, am not as I was.

Philomena—July 25, 1996

Knock on the sky and listen to the sound.

ZEN SAYING

IT HAD BEEN EXACTLY ONE YEAR TO THE DAY since my dear friend Philomena died. Neal, her husband, asked if I would join him that summer morning on the beach to scatter some of her ashes. Phil had specified exactly where she wanted her ashes spread: Central Park, Fire Island, Paris, the South of France—four wonderful healing journeys she had left for Neal. The fifth and last spot is a beach a mile from our respective homes. Neal had traveled to Central Park and Fire Island, thus far, but not yet to their local "spot." We had talked about marking the end of this first year since her death by taking Phil to the beach she so loved in life.

We had no set plan. On his way to meet me, Neal picked up some flowers. He had some of her ashes in a beautiful cobalt-blue bottle. As we followed the path the three of us (in different groupings) had so often walked during those last two years of her life, we tossed the flowers into the surf. We talked. We shared stories. We laughed a lot at Phil's wonderful antics and marveled at her wisdom and courage in living her dying and in enjoying every single moment of those last years. We silently marveled at how much she remains with us. As we began our return journey, the surf brought the flowers back to the shore. As we passed each one, Neal sprinkled some of Phil's ashes on the flower and tossed it back to sea.

It was a sweet and deeply satisfying ritual that created itself simply out of our presence and our intention. We showed up to honor our love and we were gifted with a beautiful ritual. Sometimes when we get so caught up in not "knowing how to" do things, we simply don't show up at all. We ask how to grieve when grieving is what happens when we don't close ourselves off to the pain of loss. We are afraid we don't know how to create ritual when ritual is what happens by setting our intent to honor our loss and then being present for what wants to unfold.

What is the point of setting our intent to create ritual? Rituals are acts performed for the purpose of raising consciousness, of becoming more aware. Rituals impart sanctity. When we set our intent to ritualize our loss, we sanctify that which was lost. A ritual can turn an ordinary event, like taking a walk, into an extraordinary gesture. Conscious ritual awakens us to the wonder and miracle of life.

Rituals have belonged to the province of religion since the beginning of time. The 1960s counterculture brought ritual out of the realm of religion with love-ins, be-ins, and sit-ins; with spontaneous rituals erupting at rock concerts and happenings; eventually with the sacred circle being reconfigured in support groups the world over. Perhaps part of our discomfort with creating rituals belongs to a past where we were taught religious ritual and not asked to create our own. Perhaps it arises out of a reluctance to approach the sacred. If we begin by focusing on what was sacred in the relationship we are honoring, we step away from the separation of loss and back into the wholeness of what and who was loved.

My friend Phil loved to walk along the beach and she loved flowers. For Neal and myself, throwing flowers into the surf as we walked Phil's favorite stretch of beach was as natural as thinking about Philomena. Rituals are what we create. When Marsha talked about her son Joel, stories about sports would abound. Watching a Blue Jays baseball game has become a ritual for Marsha. When Barbara's husband died, continuing the twice-yearly retreats to the

Southwest was incredibly painful but also a way to honor her love and her grief. Waking each morning to hike their favorite canyon asked a great deal of Barbara in those first few years after Steve's unexpected death but it forged an ongoing ritual that she shares more lightly and happily today with friends and family. One day Nathalie called to talk about creating a ritual to honor the first anniversary of her dad's death. Her two children were home from elementary school for the holidays and they thought they might take a picnic to the cemetery . . . or go fishing off the pier, which grandpa loved to do . . . or maybe hike through the state park. Did this sound like a good idea? Absolutely.

There are aspects of grieving that are personal and aspects that are shared. There are aspects of grieving that live in our hearts and minds and have no need of expression. And there are aspects of grieving that call for, yearn for, expression. That is the moment we turn to ritual.

The Edge

Come to the edge, he said.
No.
Come to the edge, he said.
No.
They came to the edge.
He pushed them
And
They flew.

APOLLINAIRE

HOW MANY TIMES HAVE WE HEARD someone say, after a profound loss: "I feel like I'm dreaming. I feel as if I am going to wake up and none of this will have happened." I hear this when any kind of deep loss has been encountered whether it be the death of a beloved, a relationship, a job, or a dream. It is one of the ways we have of protecting ourselves from being overwhelmed by the intensity of the loss.

We need time to reconstitute ourselves after a loss. Not only has there been a death of someone or something in our life, but we too have died a death. It is not only the person, place, or thing with whom we had the relationship that is no longer present, but the person we thought ourselves to be is also gone. We need time to think and feel and be in this world without what we have come to identify with as ordinary reality.

Loss defies us to remain complacent. It challenges us to see whether we are still the person we believed we were before this moment. Does the loss of this person or this aspect of our lives mean that we are no longer who we thought we were? How often have I heard the cry in the face of loss: "I don't know who I am anymore." This loss has brought us to the very edge of our world and we're not sure on which side of the divide we want to be. While we're deciding, we are living in nonordinary reality. Hence this feeling of being in a dream. Ordinary reality is how our lives were without this destruction, before we were dismembered. Nonordinary reality blurs the boundaries between past, present, and future. In nonordinary reality how we see, think, and feel is unfamiliar. What we believed would not or could not happen has happened. What else is subject to change? What can we trust? What are the beliefs that will stand up to these changing times?

When reality begins to shift, we slow down and start asking questions. Stop, look, listen. Those three words we were taught when we first set out to explore the world alone still apply. When we find ourselves on unfamiliar turf, we need to stop. We need to look for signs that will give us the information we need to continue on our path. "Ask and ye shall receive, seek and ye shall find." Listen. What are you hearing? More questions than answers, likely. The poet Rainer Maria Rilke exhorted us: "Live the questions now!" What are the central questions of loss? A Buddhist teacher lies dying. His students are gathered around him weeping and wondering what they will do after he is gone. Laughing, the Roshi asks: "Where am I going?"

Loss cuts us off from all of our habitual ways of thinking and just being is exhausting. Questioning tires us out and takes so much time. Grief awakens us to a new sense of time. Suddenly we have a relationship to time that is disconcerting and demanding. Time, which was a more or less predictable progression of events, now separates us from what we feel has been lost. We struggle to cross and recross that moment of time before the loss and after the loss. Often we find ourselves sleeping a great deal. This is one of the body's great healings. Sleep. Even Shakespeare understood this: "Sleep that knits up the ravell'd sleeve of care." Time and the time healing requires cannot be circumvented. Just as we cannot pull on the grass to make it grow, we can't manipulate the time it will take each of us to heal.

In sleep we encounter what tribal cultures call the Dream Time, which is a space of deep inner healing. To the dreamer the dream is absolutely real. In the days, weeks, and months following a loss, we dream about that loss. Many of us don't know how to remember our dreams or are afraid of what we might recall. Whether we remember our dreams or not, they are bringing us back into connection with what or who we are missing. We awaken from those dreams with a deep sense of well-being having visited with a part of our lives we thought lost to us forever. Contrary to what we might fear, dreaming about something or someone we are missing fills a very real need in our psyche. When Marsha dreams about Joel she always reports feeling happy, satisfied, and as if she had received a gift with their visit. Even if it is a disturbing dream, she has spent time with her son.

Dreams are gifts to be enjoyed on many levels; once we decide we are interested in our dreams, we usually begin to remember them. Setting aside extra time for rest and sleep is important when we are grieving. Too often well-meaning family, friends, and colleagues want us to keep busy and keep moving as if that will keep us safe from our pain. It won't. The only thing to keep us safe from our pain is the pain itself. "Learn how to suffer and you shall be able not to suffer." We might as well make time and room for our pain. When we set aside time to reflect quietly, time to allow our pain to talk to us, we let our grief take us where it will. We contain the grief within so that when it jumps out at us, we can say quietly: "Not now. We will have our time tonight or this afternoon." Knowing when you will sit with your grief allows you to choose a place of comfort, a safe haven.

Sometimes we fall, like Alice, down the rabbit hole. One minute we're sitting at our desks and the next moment we're plunged down into an abyss so deep and dark we fear we'll never get out. We've crossed over into nonordinary reality again. Stop—breathe. Look—where are you (emotionally)? Listen—what are you hearing? There is wisdom in taking time-out after a profound loss to stop all ordinary activity and live in this nonordinary time and space. There is wisdom in taking the time to share your story and talk about what you are experiencing with family and friends. There is wisdom in marking this loss because it is yours and will be yours as long as you live. The more time we give to this journey the more potential we have for healing through our loss so that the best of what was continues on in us.

I remember hiking with my friend Patricia the day after our friend Harvey died. We were in the Catalina Mountains outside of Tucson in late spring. We hiked silently for a long time. I was vividly aware of light, colors, smells, and shapes. I felt that life had suddenly come much more clearly into focus almost as if I were in a drug-induced state. Was it because we were touching the edge between two worlds—our world and the world into which our friend had "crossed over," the unknown realm? We too were experiencing an unknown realm; the realm in which both our friend and an important part of our ordinary lives was changing form.

I have heard William Brugh Joy, MD, speak of scientists who, by measuring sound vibrations, know that the caterpillar in the cocoon is shrieking! Screaming in pain as its body changes form from the caterpillar—a lowly creature, to most senses—to the beloved and beautiful butterfly. The butterfly is used in many traditions as a symbol of transformation and especially transmutation through death. Yet, in our highly romanticized versions, we do not acknowledge that transformation is a painful process. Painful but not fatal. Reassure yourself that, like Alice in Wonderland, you have fallen through a rabbit hole into a totally different reality. Things look the same but they aren't. They sound the same but they aren't. You don't recognize yourself. You are not crazy. You are in an unfamiliar landscape. And there you need to trust yourself and your instincts just as if you were "lost." Send out flares and stay put. Help is on its way.

Faith

Our faith is capable of reaching the realm of mystery.

UNKNOWN

LOSS WEARS MANY MASKS. For some of us, the first mask of loss we see is that of betrayal. "This wasn't supposed to happen!" Not only was this loss not in our plans but it is inconceivable to us. Most losses come at us suddenly, unexpectedly, and even if we have had time to "prepare" ourselves, as during a lengthy illness or through a drawn-out process of divorce or relocation, we still often find the reality paralyzing. We look for someone to blame: a doctor, a bus driver, a lunatic, God, ourselves. Each one is a pitfall since to place blame means that someone could have done something differently so that there would have been a different outcome. Our minds scream, "It wasn't meant to happen like this!" According to whom? The Chilean poet Pablo Neruda said, "Life is what happens while we're busy making other plans."

Our thoughts—what we are thinking—affect not only how we feel but also keep us open or closed to the possibilities inherent in any situation. Thoughts are physical energy that have been formed by consciousness. The challenge is to be conscious of those thoughts so that we are in charge of them rather than having our thoughts in charge of us. For instance: If I have a friend who betrays me, and all I can think is that she is a bad person and I am a poor victimized soul, not only will I be blind to all the factors leading up to the betrayal but I will also be blind to many of the roads leading away from the betrayal. I will be locked inside a prison of my own making!

The greatest betrayal in Judeo-Christian history, the betrayal of Jesus by Judas Iscariot, can be seen as the venality of one man selling his teacher and friend for fifty shekels or as two men in a drama that would reverberate through the ages. Whatever the circumstances or the degree of the betrayal, every situation is like an onion skin with many, many layers, and our task is to stay present as long as it takes to peel away as many of those layers as possible. In this process there is always a teaching. It is rarely the one we thought we signed up for and often one we never would have chosen but in matters of the heart and soul, we are often not consulted. If we can hold onto the idea that every moment in our lives is potentially teaching us something, we can hold ourselves open instead of collapsing around our pain, suffering, and sense of betrayal.

One morning I received, in rapid succession, two letters and a phone call from three friends whom I had always felt to be trusted allies and advisors. For twenty years I had held each of them, with their trials and tribulations, in my heart and mind, available at any hour of the day or night should they need me. Now I was in need. Struggling and vulnerable, I had turned to each of them for help. Each, for their own reasons, turned away from me. A sense of grief and betrayal threatened to overwhelm me in my already fragile state. The loss of twenty years of faith and trust that these friends would be there for me was devastating. Knowing that sixty years of relationship were crumbling beneath my feet, all I could think was, who could I trust? What is there left to trust?

The phone rang again. I picked it up. It was a wise woman friend who received my pain and loss, and said quietly to me: trust includes betrayal. In the moment she uttered those words, I knew they were true. If I tried to explain it, even to myself, I couldn't have but I could feel the wisdom, the truth, of the teaching. Over time I have struggled to learn about the trust that includes betrayal. To trust completely is to hold our faith (in that which we trust) so firmly that even what appears to be and feels like a betrayal can be included as part of the wholeness of that faith. What is such a faith? Faith that life is not arbitrarily singling us out to harass and punish us, to wound us, to torment us; faith that somewhere along the line the wisdom of this moment (of loss) will be revealed to us. Faith that this is part of the plan. Is betrayal revealed wisdom concealed?

Abraham Heschel wrote, "To have faith is not to capitulate but to rise to a higher plane of thinking. To have faith is not to defy human reason but rather to share divine wisdom."

Life in its very nature is unpredictable. There are no guarantees of what will happen next. The Tibetans say: "Tomorrow or the next life, which comes first we cannot know." That very unpredictability holds loss at its center. What we need and have today might no longer be ours tomorrow. This gives rise to the question of whether it was "ours" to begin with. Our culture and even our world has become so disconnected from the nature of life that we have come to believe that we can take possession and control it. Technology and science have seduced us into a false sense of dominance. We speak of "fighting" death and "giving" life. We speak of our "unalienable rights . . . to life, liberty and the pursuit of happiness." Is life a right or a gift, a possibility? Do we give life and can we decide when it will end?

Trust in the ebb and flow of life is essential to our well-being. We trust that the tides will rise and fall, that the sun will come up each morning, and the seasons will follow each other. Can we trust that there is meaning and wisdom in the ebb and flow, the gifts and losses, of our lives? And can we include the betrayal (of our faith) in that trust? Loss brings us to our knees. Faith in our constantly changing fortunes—trust in our singular life force raises us up again.

How big can we get in the face of this betrayal? How big can we open the lens of our minds and hearts as we look at the devastation that our lives appear to be? What would it take to keep our hearts and minds open? Betrayal is a powerful threat to our survival. In the face of betrayal we think we must bolt all the doors and windows: We must find out who the betrayer is! We close our hearts and minds at the very moment when we need more than anything to stay open to let in the love and wisdom that life also offers in the face of loss.

Loss brings us closer to the love we had and still have (where could it go?) than ever before. Because we can only feel loss for that which was cherished, the loss itself connects us to the love. And love heals. In the breaking apart we feel in the face of loss—the dismemberment—love makes us whole again.

The seed of trust lies in knowing we didn't lose what we had; that nothing can be lost once it is in our hearts and minds. The healing that the loss brings allows us to stay open in "good faith" in the presence of the betrayal of that loss. We stand in gale force winds buffeted by the duality of betrayal and trust. At the center, our hearts stand open being held by the love that created us. With love, we begin to honor the life that moves through us and that will enable us to continue living this relationship we so cherished, in new ways. We endure the pain that we, as laboring beings, must endure to bring forth new life.

It won't be easy. Life and love ask everything of us. Ultimately, they ask us to be willing to trust enough to continue loving in the face of the betrayal that loss brings.

The Gateless Gate

Man can learn nothing
except by going from
the known to the unknown.

CLAUDE BERNARD

THE KABBALAH is the mystical foundation of Judaism. It reveals how we can receive the teachings that life makes constantly available to us. In Hebrew the word Kabbalah literally means "that which is received." The Kabbalah instructs us on how to receive the lessons that are meant to help us heal our own vessel so that we, in turn, can help heal the vessel of the world.

Poetic language but what does it mean? How does it work?

Once long ago I asked my eldest brother Steven, who is himself a Kabbalist, how he would describe what a Kabbalist "does." Although Steven was always reluctant to answer my questions about this secret and highly esoteric teaching, that time he answered: "The job of a Kabbalist is Tikkun Olam, healing the world." He went on, all too briefly, to explain that all of creation is contained within a fabric, a covering, of divinity and that the responsibility of a Kabbalist is to heal any tears in the fabric. As I hung up the phone I was struck by these two words: tears and tears. Are "tears" what we shed when we feel the "tears" in the fabric of our world torn apart by loss?

When all of creation is viewed as a vessel for the divine spark of life, our mission is to keep our vessel whole, intact, so that we can contain this divine spark without having it seep away through the cracks and fissures, the tears, of everyday living. When someone or something dies, its vessel shatters and the divine spark contained within it is dispersed into the universe. When that loss is part of our lives, our vessel shatters as well. What was contained in our physical reality is now no longer contained. We have been thrown out of the physical into "metaphysical" realms by the tearing of the fabric of our known world.

The metaphysical world lives beyond the boundaries of the physical world. The prefix "meta" means something has been changed or transferred: a friendship or a marriage or a career that has ended changes from the physical relationship we had with it into a metaphysical relationship that we might continue to have with it in our memories, our thoughts, our longings, our momentoes, and even in our pain. There is usually no need to explore metaphysical reality until we experience the loss of some cherished or familiar part of our world that we don't want to let go. How do we continue to hold onto what was precious to us without a vessel? How do we transfer a relationship from the physical to the metaphysical realms?

A client told me that her grandson, whose mother had recently died, wanted to die so that he could be with his mother. Tell him, I said, that he doesn't need to die to be with his mom. Tell him that he can be with her right here, right now.

Loss is an experience that virtually begs us to walk out of the narrowness of physical experience into the wide open spaces of mystery. A mystical experience, the experience of mystery, is a moment of pure undiluted awareness. A moment where we are so fully present that nothing is pulling our attention away. When we encounter the loss of someone or something that has been a vital part of our world, nothing else matters. Not our health, not our riches, not our possibilities of recovery. All we can contain, all we choose to contain, is the pure awareness of this loss. It is at this moment that we have joined hands with the mystics. It is in this moment of pure awareness (of our loss) that we are connected to life in its biggest sense. Life is constantly renewing itself through loss.

Shari, a sixteen-year-old, wrote these words, visualized these images, after her brother died:

You Did Not Die

You live in the beautiful wind that blows
You live in the sound of birds that crow
You live in the sun that shines so bright
You live in the peaceful dark at night
You live in a star I see in the sky
You live in the ocean waves that come in with the tide
You live in the smell of flowers and grass
You live in the summer that goes so fast
You live in my heart that hurts so much
You did not die, we only lost touch.

Loss is a call into mysticism, into spirituality, because our relationship to ourselves and to our world has transcended its boundaries. Our vessel has been shattered, the fabric of our world torn, and we either take up the call to healing or collapse in despair. Grieving is either a creative act—something is born from it—or it destroys. What we want to hear, what we need to hear in the depth of our despair is the call to healing. And when we are being carried along by the ecstasy of healing, we need to remember our despair.

Using a mundane image, one of my teachers used to say that when we are healing we sometimes need to "change the channel." While we're caught up by the program on one network, all the other stations are simultaneously broadcasting their shows. Similarly, our minds also have several channels and when we find ourselves caught by the fear channel or the anger channel, we might remind ourselves that there is other programming available. Occasionally we might even need to bring ourselves back to the grief channel.

Metaphysics and mysticism might be broadcast on the wisdom channel. Do we know how to find it? What is the frequency in your part of the world for universal wisdom? Sometimes all we need to do is to let the tuner search. Listen as the tuner in your heart and soul, the mystical metaphysical ranges of your being, searches for the wisdom station. You will always recognize it. It will be crystal clear. No static. It doesn't need credentials or familiar packaging. You will know wisdom in the moment you sense it.

However, to encounter this wisdom, this guidance, the "receiver" must be sensitive enough to pick up the transmission. The vessel must be "whole" enough to search. We must be "turned on" to receive. The Kabbalah teaches that when the heart breaks, it breaks open. It breaks open to allow us to include more than the loss, more than the pain and betrayal. It breaks open to suggest that we can go beyond the limits of who we (believed we) were by meeting life through loss.

Abraham Heschel, the mystic, wrote: "Between the dawn of childhood and the door of death man encounters things and events out of which comes a whisper of truth not much louder than stillness but exhorting and persistent."

There is no stillness louder than the stillness at the heart of loss. Once, at a seminar on grief, I spoke of the idea of blessing our sorrow when we come face to face with it. At the break a young woman came up to me and told me that her little girl had died some months before and she was horrified by the idea of blessing her sorrow. She left before I could share with her that it is not sorrow we are blessing but our ability to meet it and through that meeting to change our sorrow and thereby change our world.

The Kabbalah teaches that there are three ways in which we can express sorrow. On the lowest level, we cry. On the second level, we are silent in our suffering. On the highest level, we turn our sorrow into song. There are parts of us that are enraged by the thought, the mere suggestion, of turning our sorrow into song or of blessing a meeting with sorrow. We might ask those parts a question: Is the measure of my love, my respect, my appreciation for what feels lost to me (best) expressed by saying "no" to the loss or by saying "yes" to the loss? Saying "no" to the loss means that the object of our loss is consigned to the realms of our pain, our sorrow, and its absence. Saying "yes" to the loss means allowing ourselves to embrace and be embraced by it. That embrace brings everything in: sorrow and joy, tears and laughter, love and loss, what was and what will yet be. By gathering the soul into focus through our intention to contain the divine spark of our aliveness, we heal the tears and the tears in the fabric of our world. We strengthen the vessel of our being through meeting sorrow and turning it into song. And perhaps in doing so, we might come to contain some fragment of the divine spark sent out into the world when the vessel of what we love was shattered.

This is the stuff of transformation and initiation. The gateless gate is a metaphor of initiation. It represents Life (with a capital L) calling to us. If we respond to Life's call, the veils of mystery that separate us from knowing the meaning and wisdom of life are briefly parted and we become initiates. Loss is such an initiation if we are willing to respond to its call. But what it asks of us is nothing less than to be willing to bless it.

The Never-Ending Story

It you want to stop then stop.
If you are seeking a time when you will be finished,
you will never be done.

TIBETAN SAYING

It's time for me to stop. There is much left to explore and deepen into as we consider healing through grief but then the first teaching that grief brought me was that we never "complete" our grieving. We are never finished with it. Our grief lives with us as long as we live.

It changes. It has rhythms. Sometimes it is present in its absence and sometimes it is absence that makes our grief present. Sometimes we are strong and fearless in the face of our grief and sometimes we are frightened and vulnerable. It is all part of the tapestry of our lives and by the very act of weaving our losses into that tapestry, we ensure that our losses are part of our wholeness. And so we heal.

Be patient toward all that is unsolved in your
heart and try to love the questions themselves.
Do not now seek the answers which cannot
be given you because you would not be able
to live them. And the point is to live everything.
(So) live the questions now . . .

RAINER MARIA RILKE

I am deeply grateful to have walked with you through these pages. If you would like, please write to me of your journey c/o The Shiva Foundation. Or just speak to me in the silence of your heart. Be Well,

Deborah

─────── *The Author* ───────

Deborah Morris Coryell has worked in the healing arts for more than thirty years and is cofounder and president of The Shiva Foundation, an organization dedicated to providing education and support for those encountering loss and death. She conceived and directed the Wellness/Education Program at Canyon Ranch in Tucson, Arizona, one of the nation's foremost and innovative health resorts. Based on a wellness model she developed, the program embraced a full spectrum of life patterns and resources that influence health including the capacity to grieve. Ms. Coryell has been instrumental in introducing the wellness model to the corporate world, where it is now being used extensively by companies. In addition, she has counseled families and individuals confronted with catastrophic life situations. Deborah is codirector of the Health & Wellness Division of King Ventures, which is currently developing integrative retreat centers along California's central coast. Ms. Coryell conducts retreats biannually at Sycamore Mineral Springs in San Luis Obispo, California.

shiva

The Shiva Foundation, a nonprofit organization, is committed to developing resources and offering support in the grieving process. These programs—which are under continuing development—are extended to individuals, families, communities, and corporations.

The Shiva Foundation
1241 Johnson Avenue #353
San Luis Obispo, California 93401
www.goodgrief.org

The Cover

From the moment I saw Michael Kenna's photographs I was captured by powerful images that seemed to see what the heart feels. *The Cob* expresses for me the essence of *Healing Through the Shadow of Loss:* a solitary, brooding, slightly forbidding path held in thrall by the glorious light just ahead. I am deeply grateful to Mr. Kenna for allowing us the use of his photograph.

—*DMC*

Books of Related Interest

Perfect Endings
A Conscious Approach to Dying and Death
by Robert Sachs

Life to Death: Harmonizing the Transition
A Holistic and Meditative Approach for Caregivers and the Dying
by Richard W. Boerstler, Ph.D., and Hulen S. Kornfeld, R.N.

Transforming Your Dragons
How to Turn Fear Patterns into Personal Power
by José Stevens

The Power of Emotion
Using Your Emotional Energy to Transform Your Life
by Michael Sky

Centering
A Guide to Inner Growth
by Sanders Laurie and Melvin Tucker

Emotional Healing through Mindfulness Meditation
Stories and Meditations for Women Seeking Wholeness
by Barbara Miller Fishman, Ph.D.

The Prophet's Way
A Guide to Living in the Now
by Thom Hartmann

The Balancing Act
Mastering the Five Elements of Success in Life, Relationships, and Work
by Sharon Seivert

Inner Traditions • Bear & Company
P.O. Box 388
Rochester, VT 05767
1-800-246-8648
www.InnerTraditions.com

Or contact your local bookseller